TURNED INSIDE OUT

RECOLLECTIONS OF A PRIVATE SOLDIER
IN THE ARMY OF THE POTOMAC

FRANK WILKESON

Introduction to the Bison Books Edition by
James M. McPherson

UNIVERSITY OF NEBRASKA PRESS

LINCOLN AND LONDON

⊛ The paper in this book meets the minimum requirements of
American National Standard for Information Sciences—Perma-
nence of Paper for Printed Library Materials, ANSI Z39.48-1984.

First Bison Books printing: 1997
Most recent printing indicated by the last digit below:
10   9   8   7   6   5   4   3   2   1

Library of Congress Cataloging-in-Publication Data
Wilkeson, Frank, b. 1848.
[Recollections of a private soldier in the Army of the Potomac]
Turned inside out: recollections of a private soldier in the Army of
the Potomac / Frank Wilkeson; introduction to the Bison Books
edition by James M. McPherson.
   p. cm.
Originally published: Recollections of a private soldier in the Army
of the Potomac. New York: Putnam's, 1886.
ISBN 0-8032-9799-8 (pbk.: alk. paper)
1. Wilkeson, Frank, b. 1848. 2. United States. Army of the
Potomac. 3. Soldiers—United States—Biography. 4. United
States—History—Civil War, 1861–1865—Personal narratives.
5. United States—History—Civil War, 1861–1865—Regimental
histories. I. Title.
E601.W68   1998
973.78'1—dc21
[B]
97-24009   CIP

Reprinted from the 1887 edition by G. P. Putnam's Sons titled
Recollections of a Private Soldier in the Army of the Potomac.

INTRODUCTION
James M. McPherson

Civil War soldiers described their first experience of combat as "seeing the elephant." This expression denoted any awesome phenomenon too powerful and fearful to describe in words. It probably derived from the exciting arrival of the circus in town with elephants bigger than any animal ever before seen. The Civil War was the biggest and most fearful experience that any generation of Americans has known. More than 620,000 soldiers lost their lives, 2 percent of the 1861 population of 32 million. If 2 percent of the American people were to die in a war fought at the end of the twentieth century, American deaths would number more than five million—a huge elephant indeed. The Civil War also did more to shape American society than any other event in the country's history. It preserved the United States as one nation, indivisible; it abolished the institution of slavery that had plagued and divided the country from the beginning; and it shifted the locus of economic and political power from the rural plantation South to the urban industrializing North.

Little wonder that surviving Civil War veterans looked back on their military service as the most intense and meaningful experience of their lives. By the 1880s many of these veterans were writing their memoirs, giving speeches about their war adventures, presenting papers to meetings of veterans' associations, and the like. At first most of these chroniclers were former officers. But as time went on, more and more enlisted men also published their recollections. They wanted to tell the story of the war not from the view of headquarters but from the perspective of the "grunts" who did most of the fighting and dying.

Among the earliest and best of these descriptions of the war in the trenches was Frank Wilkeson's *Recollections of a Private Soldier*, reprinted here for the first time in a modern edition. The new title reflects one of the most graphic images in the book: the pockets of dead soldiers turned inside out by battlefield ghouls who robbed the dead. Wilkeson's account is unusual in several respects, but all the more vivid because of its untypicality. Most Union volunteers had enlisted in 1861 or 1862; their average age was twenty-four. Wilkeson enlisted at the end of 1863 when he was not yet sixteen years old, putting him in a category of less than one-half of one percent of Union soldiers who were officially under the age of seventeen. Most soldier memoirs tended to glorify or romanticize their youthful experiences. Not so with Wilkeson. His narrative is starkly realistic, almost naturalistic in its portrayal of the repulsive, gruesome scenes of death, pain, suffering, filth, stupidity, cruelty, and cowardice, as well as the nobler traits of courage and dedication.

Wilkeson's opening pages plunge the reader into a sordid world of greed and inhumanity. Too young to enlist in the early years of the war (and probably lying about his age when he *did* enlist), Wilkeson was one of the few genuine volunteers who entered the Union army in the last two years of the war. By then, nearly all of the men who volunteered for patriotic reasons were already in the army. In 1863 Congress enacted conscription for the first time in American history (the Confederacy had done so a year earlier). A drafted man could hire a substitute to go in his place if he could afford it. The draftees and substitutes who began coming into the Union army in late 1863 were generally a sorry lot. But even worse were the "bounty volunteers"—men who enlisted solely for money. Under the conscription law a county could escape the draft if it could fill its quota of soldiers with volunteers. To stimulate the requisite number of volunteers, localities and states offered ever-larger bounties. This policy generated not only unreliable mercenary soldiers but also a notorious class of "bounty jumpers" who enlisted in one district, collected the bounty, and promptly deserted to do the same in another district—some of them several times.

The veterans of 1861 and 1862 universally expressed contempt for the conscripts, substitutes, and bounty men of 1863 and 1864. Their contemporary comments in letters and diaries anticipated Wilkeson's descriptions in his *Recollections*. The bounty men, wrote Union veterans in 1864, were the "off-scourings of northern slums . . . dregs of every nation . . . branded felons . . . thieves, burglars, and vagabonds." A veteran private in the 85th New York, describing the same type of men whom Wilkeson encountered on his first days in the army, commented that "those *money* soldiers are not worth as much as they cost for when you hear firing ahead you may see them hide in the woods." A division commander agreed that the new recruits of 1864 "are far inferior to the old patriotic volunteers. . . . One of the old is worth ten of the new."

When Wilkeson finally reaches his unit at the front, the 11th New York Battery, the tone of his narrative changes. Now he is among fighting veterans, whose combat record he praises. But the grim realism of the narrative pulses forward in a stark and uncompromising manner. Wilkeson experienced only seven weeks of combat with the Army of the Potomac. But those seven weeks, from the Wilderness to Petersburg in May and June 1864, saw the most intense and continuous fighting of any period in the war. At the end of this time some sixty-five thousand soldiers in the Army of the Potomac were dead, wounded, or captured. Many of the latter would die at Andersonville and other prisons. The fighting spirit of this army did not recover for eight months.

No one has described this campaign better than Wilkeson. The historians Bruce Catton and Shelby Foote relied heavily on his narrative for some of their best material in the prize-winning books *A Stillness at Appomattox* and *The Civil War: A Narrative*, vol. 3, *Red River to Appomattox*. Wilkeson's account of encountering the skeletons of men killed a year earlier at Chancellorsville on the eve of his own baptism of fire at the Wilderness, his portrayal of skulking "coffee boilers" behind Union lines, his description of the "news-gatherers" who relayed information from one unit of the army to another—all have become indelibly imprinted on our image of Civil War combat.

The reader should be forewarned, however, that Wilkeson's *Recollections* sometime have the defect of their virtues. That is, while his grimly realistic account of soldier life is a valuable corrective of the romanticization in many Civil War memoirs, Wilkeson sometimes leans too far to the dark and ugly side, producing distortions of his own. For example, his statement that four thousand men in two brigades of VI Corps were captured in a Confederate flank attack at the Wilderness is wildly inflated—the actual number was six hundred. He exaggerates the number of Union casualties at the Wilderness and Spotsylvania by 35 percent. And then there is his opinion of officers, especially generals. From time immemorial, enlisted men have complained of incompetent, sadistic, or cowardly officers. We can grant Wilkeson a license to grouse in this time-honored fashion. But when he points out that only 7 or 8 percent of the total Union killed and wounded were officers, the reader who is aware that about 6 percent of the total personnel were officers will recognize that these data prove the opposite of the point Wilkeson is trying to make. In reality, officers suffered a higher ratio of combat casualties than enlisted men, and generals experienced the highest ratio of all—50 percent greater than privates. In light of these facts, Wilkeson's contemptuous opinion of most Union generals and his assertion that he never saw one on the front lines need to be taken with more than a grain of salt.

Frank Wilkeson had a greater variety of war experiences than just about any other soldier of his age or length of service. After transferring from the 11th New York Battery to the 4th U.S. Artillery in June 1864, he participated in the defense of Washington against Jubal Early's Confederate raid in July. His unit was then sent to the prison camp at Elmira, New York, where Wilkeson's role in suppressing a riot of Confederate POW's by firing a shot into the barracks without orders got him transferred once more, to Tennessee. His description of Unionist refugees in East Tennessee, whose homes had been burned and husbands killed by Confederate soldiers and guerrillas, makes it clear that Confederate civilians were not the only Southerners to suffer from enemy occupation. Yet at no time does Wilkeson express anger or bitterness toward the enemy. Quite the contrary, he admires its fighting skills and persistence.

Few participants have evinced the grimy reality and tragedy of the Civil War better than Wilkeson. In lucid and at times gripping but always matter-of-fact prose, his account of the bloody road south from the Wilderness to Petersburg will keep readers on the edge of their seats.

CONTENTS.

PREFACE.

THE history of the fighting to suppress the slave-holders' rebellion, thus far written, has been the work of commanding generals. The private soldiers who won the battles, when they were given a chance to win them, and lost them through the ignorance and incapacity of commanders, have scarcely begun to write the history from their point of view. The two will be found to differ materially. The epauletted history has been largely inspired by vanity or jealousy, saving and excepting forever the immortal record, Grant's dying gift to his countrymen, which is as modest as it is truthful, and as just as it is modest.

Most of this war history has been written to repair damaged or wholly ruined military reputations. It has been made additionally untrustworthy by the jealousy which seeks to belittle the work of others, or to falsify or obscure it, in order to render more conspicuous the achievements of the historians. The men who carried the muskets, served the guns, and rode in the saddle had no military reputations to defend or create, and they brought not out of the war professional jealousy of their comrades. They and they alone can supplement the wonderful contribution made by Grant to the history of the struggle to suppress the rebellion. Who beside the enlisted men can tell how the fierce Confederates looked and fought behind their earthworks and in the open; how the heroic soldiers of the impoverished South were clothed, armed, and fed? Who beside our enlisted men can or will tell their countrymen how the volunteers who saved the republic lived in camp; lived in the field; on the march; what they talked about; how they criticised the campaigns, and criticised their officers and commanders; how oft they hungered and thirsted; how, through parts of campaigns, and through entire campaigns, they slept unsheltered on the ground, and too often in snow or mud; how they fought (honor and glory for ever and ever to these matchless warriors!) and how they died?

I was one of these private soldiers. As one of them, I make this my contribution to the true history of the war. And I call on those of my comrades in the ranks who yet survive, in whatever part of the country they served, to make haste to leave behind them as their contributions, what they actually saw and did, and what their commanders refused, or neglected or failed to do. Very many of you were the equals, and not a few of you were the superiors, of your officers in intelligence, courage, and military ability. Your judgment about the conduct of the war, by reason of the vastness of your number, will have the force of public opinion. That is almost invariably right. The opinion of the rank and file of an army of Americans will be equally right. The grumbling of a single soldier at a camp fire may be unreasonable and his criticism abusive. The criticism of 100,000 American soldiers will be absolute truth.

I am conscious of imperfect performance of the task I set to myself in the writing of this book. In a later edition I hope to have the opportunity to correct my short-coming. Moderation and forbearance of statement and opinion have been my error. Occasionally I ceased to write as a soldier in the ranks. Too frequently I wrote as a generous narrator a quarter of a century after the events. I ought to have written from title-page to cover as if I were still in the ranks. And the limited compass of the book forbade the consideration of two subjects about which I feel deeply, and which I propose hereafter to treat with what strength I possess. For much thinking over my experience as a private in the Army of the Potomac has confirmed me in the belief I then entertained, that the two capital errors in the conduct of the war on the Union side were ;

First. The calling for volunteers to suppress the rebellion, instead of at the outset creating armies by drawing soldiers ratably and by lot from the able-bodied population, between the ages of twenty and forty, of all the free States and territories.

Second. The officering of the commands in the various armies with West Point graduates by preference, on the assumption that they knew the art of war and were soldiers, and were therefore the fittest to command soldiers.

It is my purpose in the future edition of this book to show how the resort to volunteering, the unprincipled dodge of cowardly politicians, ground up the choicest seed-corn of the nation ; how it consumed the young, the patriotic, the intelligent, the generous, the brave ; how it wasted the best moral, social, and political elements of the republic, leaving the cowards, shirks, egotists, and money-makers to stay at home and procreate their kind ; how the Lexingtons being away in the war, the production of Lexington colts ceased.

Again, I carried out with me from the ranks, not only the feeling, but the knowledge derived from my own experience and from the current history of the war, that the military salvation of this country requires that the West Point Academy be destroyed. Successful commanders of armies are not made. Like great poets they are born. Men like Cæsar, Marlborough, Napoleon, and Grant are not the products of schools. They occur sparingly in the course of nature. West Point turns out shoulder-strapped office-holders. It cannot produce soldiers ; for these are, as I claim, born, and not made. And it is susceptible of demonstration that the almost ruinous delay in suppressing the rebellion and restoring the Union ; the deadly failure of campaigns year after year ; the awful waste of the best soldiers the world has seen ; and the piling up of the public debt into the billions, was wholly due to West Point influence and West Point commanders. They were commanders, but they were not soldiers.

FRANK WILKESON.

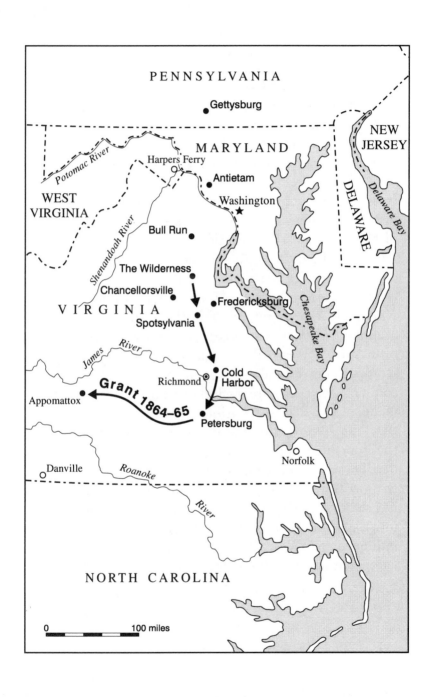

PENNSYLVANIA

● Gettysburg

MARYLAND

Potomac River

Harpers Ferry ○

● Antietam

WEST
VIRGINIA

★ Washington

Shenandoah River

Bull Run ●

NEW
JERSEY

DELAWARE

Delaware Bay

The Wilderness ●

Chancellorsville ●

VIRGINIA

Spotsylvania ●

● Fredericksburg

Chesapeake Bay

James River

Grant 1864–65

Richmond ◎

● Cold
Harbor

Appomattox ●

● Petersburg

Danville ○

Roanoke

● Norfolk

River

NORTH CAROLINA

0   100 miles

RECOLLECTIONS OF A PRIVATE.

I.

FROM BARRACKS TO FRONT.

I WAS a private soldier in the war to suppress the rebellion. I write of the life of a private soldier. I gloss over nothing. The enlisted men, of whom I was one, composed the army. We won or lost the battles. I tell how we lived, how we fought, what we talked of o' nights, of our aspirations and fears. I do not claim to have seen all of Grant's last campaign ; but what I saw I faithfully record.

The war fever seized me in 1863. All the summer and fall I had fretted and burned to be off. That winter, and before I was sixteen years old, I ran away from my father's highlying Hudson River valley farm. I went to Albany and enlisted in the Eleventh New York Battery, then at the front in Virginia, and was promptly sent out to the penitentiary building. There, to my utter astonishment, I found eight hundred or one thousand ruffians, closely guarded by heavy lines of sentinels, who paced to and fro, day and night, rifle in hand, to keep them from running away. When I entered the barracks these recruits gathered around me and asked, "How much bounty did you get?" "How many times have you jumped the bounty?" I answered that I had not bargained for any bounty, that I had never jumped a bounty, and that I had enlisted to go to the front and fight. I was instantly assailed with abuse. Irreclaimable blackguards, thieves, and ruffians gathered in a boisterous circle around me and called me foul names. I was robbed while in these barracks of all I possessed—a pipe, a piece of tobacco and a knife. I remained in this nasty prison for a month. I became thoroughly acquainted with my comrades. A recruit's social standing in the barracks was determined by the acts of villany he had performed, supplemented by the number of times he had jumped the bounty. The social standing of a hard-faced, crafty pickpocket, who had jumped the bounty in say half a dozen cities, was assured. He shamelessly boasted of

his rascally agility. Less active bounty-jumpers looked up to him as to a leader. He commanded their profound respect. When he
talked, men gathered around him in crowds
and listened attentively to words of wisdom
concerning bounty-jumping that dropped from
his tobacco-stained lips. His right to occupy
the most desirable bunk, or to stand at the head
of the column when we prepared to march to
the kitchen for our rations, was undisputed. If
there was a man in all that shameless crew who
had enlisted from patriotic motives, I did not
see him. There was not a man of them who
was not eager to run away. Not a man who
did not quake when he thought of the front.
Almost to a man they were bullies 'and cowards, and almost to a man they belonged to
the criminal classes.

I had been in this den of murderers and
thieves for a week, when my uncle William
Wilkeson of Buffalo found me. My absence
from the farm had caused a search of the New
York barracks to be made for me. My uncle,
finding that I was resolute in my intention to
go to the front, and that I would not accept a
discharge, boy as I was, did the best thing he
could for me, and that was to vouch for me to

the major, named Van Rensselaer, I think, who was in charge of the barracks. He knew my family, and when he heard that I had run away from home to enlist, and that I would not accept a discharge, he gave me the freedom of the city. I had a pass which I left in charge of the officer of the guard when not using it, because I was afraid I would be robbed of it if I took it into the barracks. The fact of my having a pass became known to the bounty-jumpers, and I was repeatedly offered large sums of money for it. In the room in which I slept, a gang of roughs made up a pot of $1,700, counting out the money before me, and offered it to me if I would go out and at night put my pass in a crack between two designated boards that formed a portion of a high fence that surrounded the penitentiary grounds. I refused to enter into the scheme, and they attacked me savagely, and would have beaten me, perhaps to death, if the guards, hearing the noise, had not rushed in. Of course they swore that I had madly assaulted them with a heavy bed slat, and, of course, I was punished, and, equally of course, I kept my mouth shut as to the real cause of the row, for fear that I would be murdered as I slept if I exposed them. In front of the barracks stood a high wooden horse, made by sticking four long poles into large holes bored into a smooth log, and then standing it upright. Two ladders, one at each end, led up to the round body of the wooden steed. A placard, on which was printed in letters four inches long the word "Fighting," was fastened on my back. Then I was led to the rear ladder and told to mount the horse and to shin along to the other end, and to sit there until I was released. The sentinel tapped his rifle significantly, and said, earnestly: "It is loaded. If you dismount before you are ordered to, I shall kill you." I believed he meant what he said, and I did not get off till ordered to dismount. For the first hour I rather enjoyed the ride ; then my legs grew heavy, my knees pained dreadfully, and I grew feverish and was very thirsty. Other men came out of the barracks and climbed aloft to join in the pleasure of wooden horseback riding. They laughed at first, but soon began to swear in low tones, and to curse the days on which they were born. In the course of three hours the log filled up, and I dismounted to make room for a fresh offender. The placard was taken from my back, and I was gruffly ordered to "get out of this." I staggered back a few yards, stooped to rub my lame knees, and looked at the gang who were sadly riding the wooden horse. Various words were printed on the cards that were fastened to their backs, but more than half of them announced that the bearers were thieves.

On my urgent solicitation Major Van Rensselaer promised to ship me with the first detachment of recruits going to the front. One cold afternoon, directly after the ice had gone out of the Hudson River, we were ordered out of the barracks. We were formed into ranks, and stood in a long, curved line 1,000 rascals strong. We were counted, as was the daily custom, to see if any of the patriots had escaped. Then, after telling us to step four paces to the front as our names were called, the names of the men who were to form the detachment were shouted by a sergeant, and we stepped to the front, one after another, until 600 of us stood in ranks. We were marched to the barracks, and told to pack our knapsacks as we were to march at once. The 400 recruits who had not been selected were carefully guarded on the ground, so as to prevent their mingling with us. If that had happened, some of the recruits who had been chosen would have failed to appear at the proper time. The idea was that if we were kept separate, all the men in the barracks, all outside of the men grouped under guard, would have to go. Before I left the barracks I saw the guards roughly haul straw-littered, dust-coated men out of mat-resses, which they had cut open and crawled into to hide. Other men were jerked out of the water-closets. Still others were drawn by the feet from beneath bunks. One man, who had burrowed into the contents of a water-tight swill-box, which stood in the hall and into which we threw our waste food and coffee slops, was fished out, covered with coffee grounds and bits of bread and shreds of meat, and kicked down stairs and out of the building. Ever after I thought of that soldier as the hero of the swill-tub. Cuffed, prodded with bayonets, and heartily cursed, we fell into line in front of the barracks. An officer stepped in front of us and said in a loud voice that any man who at-tempted to escape would be shot. A double line of guards quickly took their proper posi-tions around us. We were faced to the right and marched through a room, where the men were paid their bounties. Some men received $500, others less ; but I heard of no man who received less than $400. I got nothing. As the men passed through the room they were formed into column by fours. When all the recruits had been paid, and the column formed, we started to march into Albany, guarded by a double line of sentinels. Long before we arrived at State Street three recruits attempted to escape. They dropped their knapsacks and fled wildly. Crack! crack! crack! a dozen rifles rang out, and what had been three men swiftly running were three bloody corpses. The dead patriots lay by the roadside as we marched by. We marched down State Street, turned to the right at Broadway, and marched down that street to the steamboat landing. Previous to my enlistment I had imagined that the population of Albany would line the sidewalks to see the defenders of the nation march proudly by, bound for the front, and that we would be cheered, and would unbend sufficiently to accept floral offerings from beautiful maidens. How was it? No exultant cheers arose from the column. The people who saw us did not cheer. The faces of the recruits plainly expressed the profound disgust they felt at the disastrous outcome of what had promised to be a remunerative financial enterprise. Small boys derided us. Mud balls were thrown at us. One small lad, who was greatly excited by the unwonted spectacle, rushed to a street corner, and after placing his hands to his mouth, yelled to a distant and loved comrade: " Hi, Johnnie, come see de bounty-jumpers!" He was promptly joined by an exasperating, red-headed, sharp-tongued little wretch, whom I desired to destroy long before we arrived at the steamboat landing. Men and women openly laughed at us. Fingers, indicative of derision, were pointed at us. Yes, a large portion of the populace of Albany gathered together to see us; but they were mostly young males, called guttersnipes. They jeered us, and were exceedingly loth to leave us. It was as though the congress of American wonders were parading in the streets preparatory to aërial flights under tented canvas.

Once on the steamboat, we were herded on the lower deck, where freight is usually carried, like cattle. No one dared to take off his knapsack for fear it would be stolen. Armed sentinels stood at the openings in the vessel's sides out of which gangplanks were thrust. Others were stationed in the bows; others in the dark narrow passage-ways where the shaft turns;

still others were on the decks. We were hemmed
in by a wall of glistening steel. " Stand back,
stand back, damn you!" was the only remark
the alert-eyed, stern-faced sentinels uttered, and
the necessity of obeying that command was
impressed on us by menacing bayonets.
Whiskey, guard-eluding whiskey, got in. Bot-
tles, flasks, canteens, full of whiskey, circulated
freely among us, and many men got drunk.
There was an orgie on the North River steamer
that night, but comparatively a decent one. In
spite of the almost certain death sure to ensue
if a man attempted to escape, two men jumped
overboard. I saw one of these take off his
knapsack, loosen his overcoat and then sit down
on his knapsack. He drew a whiskey flask from
an inner pocket and repeatedly stimulated his
courage. He watched the guards who stood by
the opening in the vessel's side intently. At
last they turned their heads for an instant. The
man sprang to his feet, dropped his overcoat
and ran to the opening and jumped far out into
the cold waters of the river. Instantly the
guards began to fire. Above us, in front of us,
at our sides, behind us, wherever guards were
stationed, there rifles cracked. But it was ex-
ceeding dark on the water, and I believe that

the deserter escaped safely. Early in the morning, before it was light, I again heard firing. I was told that another recuit had jumped overboard and had been killed.

In this steamboat were two mysterious men clad in soldiers' clothing, whom I had not seen until after we left Albany. Their appearance was so striking, they were so alert and quick-eyed, so out of place among us, that my attention was attracted to them. One of these men was an active, trim built, dark-eyed, black-haired, handsome fellow of 25 years. The other was a stocky, red-faced blonde of about 30. They moved quickly among the recruits. They made pleasant, cheerful remarks to almost every man on the steamboat. They told stories which were greatly enjoyed by the recruits who heard them. "Where did those two men join us? Where did they come from, and who are they?" were questions I musingly asked myself over and over and over again, as I sat on my knapsack in a corner. Finally I walked to a guard and asked who they were. He eyed me suspiciously for an instant, and then furiously answered: "Stand back, you bounty-jumping cur!" and he lunged at me with his bayonet as though to thrust me through. I stood back, and then I sat down on my knapsack in a corner and wondered musingly if I were a patriot or simply a young fool.

Morning came, and we disembarked in New York, and were marched, still heavily guarded, to the low, white barracks, which then stood where the post-office now stands. There we were securely penned and decently fed. The men fretted and fumed, and burned to escape. Many of them had previously jumped bounties in New York. They knew the slums of the city. They knew where to hide in safety. Dozens of them said that if they could get out of the barracks they would be safe. But they could not get out. This time they were going to the front. The officers and men, in whose charge we were, were resolute in their intention to deliver one consignment of bounty-jumpers to the commands they belonged to. That afternoon five days' cooked rations were issued to us, and we were escorted by a heavy double line of guards down Broadway to the Battery. There we turned to march along a street that led to a dock where an ocean steamer lay. The head of the column was opposite the dock, when four recruits shed their knapsacks and ran for the freedom they coveted. One of these men

marched two files in front of me. He dashed
past the guard, who walked by my side, at the
top of his speed. Not a word was said to him.
The column halted at command. The guard
near me turned on his heels quickly, threw his
heavy rifle to his shoulder, covered the running
man, and shot him dead. Two of the remain-
ing three fell dead as other rifles cracked. The
fourth man ran through the shower of balls
safely. I thought he was going to escape; but
a tall, lithe officer ran after him, pistol in hand.
He overtook the fugitive just as he was about
to turn a street corner. He made no attempt
to arrest the deserter, but placed his pistol to
the back of the runaway's head and blew his
brains out as he ran. The dead man fell in a
pile at the base of a lamp-post. That ended
all attempts to escape. We marched on board
the steamer, a propeller, and descended narrow
stairs to between decks, where the light was
dim and the air heavy with a smell as of damp
sea-weed. There were three large hatches,
freight hatches probably, in the deck above us,
through which the heavy, cold, outside air sank,
and through which three systems of draughty,
sneeze-provoking ventilation were established
as soon as the air in the hold became heated.

Tobacco smoke arose from hundreds of pipes and cheap cigars, and the air grew hazy. At short distances the forms of men were indistinct and phantom-like. In this space were about 600 men. False history and dishonest Congressmen who desire to secure re-election by gifts of public money and property to voters, say they were brave Northern youth going to the defence of their country. I, who know, say they were as arrant a gang of cowards, thieves, murderers, and blacklegs as were ever gathered inside the walls of Newgate or Sing Sing.

Money was plentiful and whiskey entered through the steamer's ports, and the guards drove a profitable business in selling canteens full of whiskey at $5 each. Promptly the hold was transformed into a floating hell. The air grew denser and denser with tobacco smoke. Drunken men staggered to and fro. They yelled and sung and danced, and then they fought and fought again. Rings were formed, and within them men pounded each other fiercely. They rolled on the slimy floor and howled and swore and bit and gouged, and the delighted spectators cheered them to redouble their efforts. Out of these fights others sprang into life, and from these still others. The noise was horrible. The wharf became crowded with men eager to know what was going on in the vessel. A tug was sent for, and we were towed into the river, and there the anchors were dropped. Guards ran in on us and beat men with clubbed rifles, and were in turn attacked. We drove them out of the hold. The hatch at the head of the stairs was closed and locked. The recruits were maddened with whiskey. Dozens of men ran a muck, striking every one they came to, and being struck and kicked and stamped on in return. The ventilation hatches were surrounded by stern-faced sentinels, who gazed into the gloom below and warned us not to try to get out by climbing through the hatches. Men sprang high in the air and clutched the hatch railings, and had their hands smashed with musket butts. Sentinels paced to and fro along the vessel's deck, and called loudly to all row-boats to keep off or they would be fired upon. They did not intend that any fresh supplies of whiskey should be brought to us. The prisoners in this floating hell were then told to " go it," and they went it. We had been searched for arms before we entered the barracks at Albany. The more decent and quiet of us had no means of killing the drunken brutes who pressed on us. There was not a club or a knife or an iron bolt that we could lay our hands to. I fought, and got licked; fought again, and won; and for the third time faced my man, and got knocked stiff in two seconds. It was a scene to make a devil howl with delight. The light grew dimmer and dimmer, and then the interior of the hold was dark, except such portions as were dimly lighted by the bars of light that shot through the ports and that which was reflected down the hatches in square columns. We fought and howled and swore with rage and pain. Through it all the smell was overpowering. The deadly, penetrating odors of ulcerous men, who suffered from unnamable diseases, of stale tobacco-smoke, the sickening fumes of dead whiskey, and the smell of many unclean ruffians made the air heavy with a horrible stench. Many recruits lost their bounty money. They were robbed and beaten almost to death. Exhaustion quieted the devils down during the night, and then we slept on the filthy floor. There was not a bunk in the entire hold. The next morning we awoke with sore heads and faint stomachs, and, under orders, washed out the vast room as well as we could. We remained in New York harbor for two days, waiting for the officer who had killed the runaway to be tried and acquitted. During the delay the guards refused to allow a row-boat to come near us. Then we started for Alexandria, in Virginia.

Shortly after we had begun to steam for the sea I saw the two alert-eyed recruits, who had attracted my attention when we were on the Hudson River steamboat, in the hold with us. I am positive that they were not with us while we lay in New York harbor. They walked among us for a couple of hours, talking pleasantly. The younger of the twain inquired kindly as to how I got my face pounded, and he got me a bowl of clean water to bathe it in. Toward noon they produced chuck-luck cloths and dice boxes, and furious gambling began. I was the only man on board who was not bounty paid or laden. I had but $10, which my father had given to me when I was in the New York barracks, so I could not join in the sport. I have seen gambling—and wild, reckless gambling too—in many mining camps, and in towns where Texas cattle were sold, and in new railroad towns beyond the Missouri ; but never since the war closed have I seen such reckless gambling as went on day and night in this vessel. Men crowded around the brace games, and speedily lost their bounties. Then the losers would boldly, in broad daylight, rob their comrades. I saw gangs of robbers knock men down and go through their pockets, and unbuckle money belts from their waists ; and if they protested, their cries were silenced with boot heels stamped into their faces.

By the time this floating hell and its cargo of cowardly devils had got into Chesapeake Bay, the two alert-eyed gamblers possessed about all the money the six hundred recruits had. Then they grew fearful of the men they had robbed, and hired some of the soldiers to guard them. I saw two soldiers paid $100 each for guarding them while they slept. Unguarded, they would have been killed and torn limb from limb. At Alexandria we, dirty and smelling so vilely that the street dogs refused to approach us, were marched to clean barracks and well fed. That evening I paid a soldier $5 to stand over a bath-tub and watch me while I bathed. I had to go outside of the barracks to bathe. The next morning the two alert-eyed gamblers were missing. I never saw them again. I knew that thcy were not recruits, but gamblers in league with high officials—gamblers carefully selected for their professional skill and pleasing address, and that they had been sent on the sea-voyage to rob the bounty-laden recruits. The trip had been exceedingly profitable. At the lowest calculation there had been $240,000 in the recruits' pockets when they left New York. I do not believe the same pockets contained $70,000 when we arrived at Alexandria.

After breakfast we were counted, and the men of each regiment separated into groups and told to keep together. We were then marched under guard to a train of box-cars, and loaded into them much as cattle are. The interior of the car filled, the recruits were piled on top. At each of the side doors of the cars stood two armed sentinels. Two more sat on top outside at each end of the car. In the end car of the train were a couple of officers and fifteen or twenty privates. On the tender of the locomotive were more guards. We were solemnly told by an officer that any man who got off the car without permission would be shot dead. Five men did not believe this statement, or they may have been so greatly appalled by the prospect of meeting Lec's soldiers, that they resolved to attempt to escape.

Be that as it may, five men jumped from the train while it was in motion, and were instantly killed by the guards. The train was stopped and their corpses were thrown into the rear car. The men in the car I was in were ordered off at Brandy Station. We fell into line and were counted, and then turned over to other guards, whose officer receipted for us. We faced into column and marched from camp to camp, and at each camp some recruits were counted out as if they were sheep, and receipted for. During this march of distribution I learned where many regiments were camped, and I often visited them before the campaign opened.

I rather enjoyed the afternoon. My knapsack was light (some patriot had stolen its contents while I slept on the steamer), the walking was good, the air was pure and sweet, the scene was novel and interesting ; and, above all, the propeller was at Alexandria. About 9 o'clock the last guard and I, now in friendly conversation about the trip from Albany to the front, arrived at the camp of the Eleventh New York Battery, and I was receipted for. The next morning I drew a full outfit of clothing and burned the befouled garments I had worn on the " Floating Heaven of American Patriots," as I named the propeller.

II.

IN CAMP AT BRANDY STATION.

DURING the winter of 1863–64 the Army of the Potomac was camped in Virginia north of the Rapidan River. A large portion of it was at Brandy Station. The enlisted men were comfortably housed in canvas-covered log huts. There was a large fireplace in each hut, and wood was abundant and to be had for the cutting. The old oak forests of Virginia, whose owners were gathered in ranks under Lee to oppose us, suffered that winter. When the weather was fit the soldiers were drilled, and drilled, and drilled again. We were well fed, having plenty of bread, fresh beef, salted pork, beans, rice, sugar, and coffee.

In front of the ground on which the battery I belonged to was camped, was a large plain. On it several regiments, in heavy marching order, were drilled every pleasant day. Instead of practising the men in the simple flank and

line movements used in battle, or at targets, or
in estimating distances, they were marched to
and fro and made to perform displayful evolu-
tions, which conveyed the impression to the
spectators that thousands of Knights Templar
were moving in competitive drill for a valuable,
and, maybe, sacred prize.   In the artillery service the drill was still more absurd.   Teams
were hitched to the guns almost daily, and they
were whirled over comparatively dry ground in
a highly bewildering but exceedingly useless
manner.   Every enlisted man in the army knew
that we were to fight in a rugged, wooded
country where the clearings were surrounded
by heavy forests, and where deep shrub and
timber-clad ravines hazed the air, and where
practice and practice and still more practice in
estimating distances was required, if we were to
fire accurately and effectively.   Did the artillery officers zealously practise us in estimating
distance ?   Never, to my knowledge.   They
taught us how to change front to the right, to
the rear, and on the several pieces that formed
the battery, which knowledge was of as much
practical use to us as if we had been assidu-
ously drilled to walk on stilts or to play on the
banjo.   Never, while I was in the artillery

camp, did I see the guns unlimber for target practice. The dismounted, or gun drill, was useful; but this, too, was loaded down with memory-clogging detail.

One night, one of the gunners named Jellet and I sat late by the hut fireplace after an afternoon's hard work at the guns, and I, young in years and service, humbly suggested that I thought that much of the drill we were being taught was absurd and useless, and that there was not time before the spring campaign opened to teach the new recruits the entire light-artillery drill. Soberly, the corporal who had sighted the gun I served on through many battles, laid his hand on my shoulder and said impressively:

" My lad, you are just beginning to discover the artillery humbug. You serve in what should be the most efficient arm of the service; an arm where men and horses and guns should be wasted as water, where tons of ammunition should be expended in target practice, because if a gunner cannot hit the object he fires at he had better not fire at all, as to miss excites the contempt of the enemy. I have served for two years in this army," he added, after an instant's pause, " and there is not a general officer in it

who understands how to use artillery, not one."
Here the corporal swore roundly, and then he
added, prophetically, as he solemnly nodded
his head : " Wait until you get into the field
and your heart will be broken." Then he went
to bed leaving me by the fire, where I sat and
toasted myself until I heard a guard approach-
ing the tent, then I turned in in full dress and
was sleeping soundly when the guard inquired
why we had a light after taps.

How tired I got of camp, and drill, and
guard duty ! And how tired I got of the rain
and mud ! A large portion of the battery men
were religious. Almost nightly these men held
a prayer-meeting. Next to us, on the right, a
battery manned by Irishmen was parked, and
almost nightly they indulged in a fist fight.
Once in a while they evinced a desire to fight
with us, and at long intervals some of the un-
regenerated men of our battery gratified them
and got whipped. Still farther to the right a
battery of the Fourth United States Artillery
was parked. The men of that command were
either Irish or Irish-Americans, and they were
keen to gratify the desire of volunteer Irish, or
any other volunteers, to indulge in personal
combat. To our left a full regiment of Ger-

mans, heavy-artillery men, were camped. Between them and the regular army artillerymen a bloody feud existed. Many and many a German was savagely beaten by the Irishmen. This regiment of Germans interested me greatly. In their camp I first saw lager beer. I bought a glass of it, but finding it a weak, sloppy drink, I left the almost full glass on the counter. So strong an impression did this first drink of lager make on me, that I never see the foamy, amber-colored liquor that the sutler's tent, standing on a muddy plain, and surrounded by stout, blue-coated Germans, does not arise before me. These Germans had a vast amount of personal property. They had recently arrived from the fortifications near Washington, and had brought their accumulated wealth with them. All of the enlisted men had one knapsack, and many of them had two, and there was a plenty of musical instruments in their camp. I used to look into my lean knapsack after a visit to the Germans, and wish it would bulge with fatness as theirs did. This regiment of Germans made more noise in their camp than two brigades of Americans would or could have done.

One day I was walking near the camp of Bat-

tery A, Fourth United States Artillery.   Some
of the men of that command were drunk, and
among them was a line sergeant, a sturdy, blue-
eyed, black-haired Scotchman.   He was wildly
drunk, but not staggering.   He had full control
of himself physically, but mentally he was a
madman.   He cursed loudly, and swaggered
with vehement gesticulation around the camp.
I saw a door of a tent thrown open and a handsome young officer stepped out.   He was neat,
erect, quick-stepping, and sharp-voiced.

"Sergeant of the guard!" he called loudly.

A sergeant stepped up and saluted.

"Put a gag in Sergeant Stewart's mouth, and
then tie him on a spare wheel and give it a
quarter turn!" the sharp-voiced officer said
loudly.

The sergeant of the guard saluted again and
turned to obey.   Stewart heard the order, and
turned without saluting and ran at the top
of his speed to a large tree that stood a few
hundred yards off on the plain.   When he
reached the tree he nimbly swung himself upward into its lower limbs, and speedily climbed
to the top.   Once there, he drew a heavy revolver and promptly opened fire on the sergeant
of the guard and his detachment.   He checked

the pursuit. Then he howled and swore, and amused himself by shooting at strange horse-men who happened to come within range. The quick-stepping, alert-eyed officer came to us and asked the cause of the delay in catching Stewart. On being answered, he walked toward the tree. Stewart emptied his revolver at him and missed him. He grasped the useless weapon by the barrel and waited until he got a fair chance, and then launched it at his offi-cer, who stepped aside to avoid it. He walked under the tree.

"Sergeant Stewart, come down!" he com-manded.

"To be tied on the wheel?" Stewart in-quired.

"Yes; to be gagged and tied on the wheel," the officer replied.

"Then I'll not come down," the sergeant resolutely said.

The officer drew his revolver, covered Stewart with it, and said sternly:

"Come down, or I will kill you."

"I'll not come down," said Stewart. You can kill me, but you cannot tie me up." And Stewart glared savagely at the officer and whooped exultantly.

The rage of the officer was intense. He lowered his revolver and swore that he would tie him on a wheel, and that he would not gratify him by killing him.

"Go to the battery wagon and bring some axes here," he said sharply to a corporal. The axes were brought and two men began to chop the tree down. Sergeant Stewart did not fancy the prospect of riding on an oak tree as it swung through the air and crashed on the earth. He began to parley. Would his officer kindly shoot him if he came down? No, he would not. Would he not order his head to be, cut off? No, he would not. Stewart descended limb by limb, and at every limb he tried to have the disgraceful sentence mitigated to death. His officer was obdurate. He was resolute in his intention to gag him and tie him on a wheel. Stewart finally sat on a lower limb. Any of the men could have taken him by the legs and pulled him down. He wanted that done. That would have been capture, not surrender. He was not gratified. He had to climb down. Then he was marched to a spare wheel and strapped on it, previously having a heavy gag thrust crossways into his mouth and bound firmly in its position. I was amazed that

Stewart had not been shot. I talked to the men and they told me that he was the best sergeant in the battery, a marvellous shot with a Napoleon gun and that his getting drunk was an accident.

" Oh," exclaimed a gray-haired private who had three service stripes on his coat sleeve," he will be court-martialled and get three years at the Dry Tortugas. Before the sentence is received here, the battery will be in the field and Stewart at his gun. The officers will not publish the order, but will hold it over him. If he again gets drunk or becomes insubordinate, then he will catch it."

When I left the camp of the regulars Stewart was hanging on the wheel and the men were drilling at the guns, and no one was paying a particle of attention to Stewart's inarticulate cries and acute suffering. Here I will say that the prediction made by the private whose coat sleeves were covered with service stripes came true. After I was promoted into the regular army I served with Battery A, Fourth Artillery, and Sergeant Stewart was then a line sergeant. He got drunk and attacked an officer with a tent pole, and the old sentence of the court which tried him at Brandy Station was put into

execution.   He was sent to the Dry Tortugas
for three years.

The discipline throughout the Army of the
Potomac during the winter of 1863–64 was
necessarily severe.   The ranks of the original
volunteers, the men who sprang to arms at the
tap of the northern war-drum, had been shot to
pieces. Entire platoons had disappeared. Regiments that had entered the great camps of in-
struction formed around Washington in 1861–
62 a thousand men strong, had melted before the
heat of Confederate battle-fire till they numbered three hundred, two hundred, and as low
as one hundred and fifty men.   During the winter of 1863–64 these regiments were being filled
with bounty-jumpers, and these men had to be
severely disciplined, and that entailed punishment.   There was no longer the friendly feeling of cordial comradeship between the enlisted
men and their officers, which was one of the
distinguishing characteristics of the volunteer
troops.   The whole army was rapidly assuming
the character and bearing of regular troops, and
that means mercenaries.   The lines drawn between the recruits of 1863–64 and their officers
were well marked, and they were rigid.   The
officers were resolute in their intention to make

the recruits feel the difference in their rank. Breaches of army discipline were promptly and severely punished. There is an unwritten military axiom which says that frequent courts-martial convened to try enlisted men for petty offences, sharply indicate that the regimental officers are inefficient. There was no complaint on this score in the Army of the Potomac in 1863–64. There was no necessity for punishing the volunteers. They were men of high intelligence. They could be reasoned with. They could and did see the necessity of soldier-like and decent behavior in their camps. They cheerfully obeyed orders, because they realized the necessity of obedience. But with large bounties came a different class of recruits, the bounty-jumpers. These men had to be heartlessly moulded into soldiers. And, while it is true that the apparently brutal methods employed to check the insolent tongues and to curb the insubordinate spirits of these men did succeed in creating the outward semblance of soldiers, it is also true that no earthly power could change the character of their hearts; and they were essentially cowardly. The bounty-jumpers would cheerfully engage in savage rows; they would fight fiercely with their fists, but they could not and did not stand battle-fire stanchly.

The punishments inflicted on the enlisted men were various, and some of them were horribly brutal and needlessly severe; but they apparently served their purpose, and the times were cruel, and men had been hardened to bear the suffering of other men without wincing. One punishment much affected in the light artillery was called " tying on the spare wheel." Springing upward and rearward from the centre rail of every caisson was a fifth axle, and on it was a spare wheel. A soldier who had been insubordinate was taken to the spare wheel and forced to step upon it. His legs were drawn apart until they spanned three spokes. His arms were stretched until there were three or four spokes between his hands. Then feet and hands were firmly bound to the felloes of the wheel. If the soldier was to be punished moderately he was left, bound in an upright position on the wheel for five or six hours. If the punishment was to be severe, the ponderous wheel was given a quarter turn after the soldier had been lashed to it, which changed the position of the man being punished from an upright to a horizontal one. Then the prisoner had to exert all his strength to keep his weight from pulling heavily and cuttingly on the cords that bound his upper arm and leg to the wheel. I have frequently seen men faint while undergoing this punishment, and I have known men to endure it for hours without a murmur, but with white faces, and set jaws and blazing eyes. To cry out, to beg for mercy, to protest, ensured additional discomfort in the shape of a gag, a rough stick, being tied into the suffering man's mouth. Tying on the spare wheel was the usual punishment in the artillery service for rather serious offences ; and no man wanted to be tied up but once.

There was another punishment which was much more severe than the spare wheel, and which, because it was apt to cripple the men physically, was very rarely employed. This was known as " tying on the rack." Back of every battery wagon is a heavy, strong rack, on which forage is carried. It stands out about two feet behind the wheels. Its edge is not over an inch thick. The soldier who was to suffer the tortures of the rack was led to it. His hands were dragged forward as far as they could be without lifting his feet from the ground, and there they were bound to the

felloes of the wheel.   Then one foot was lifted
and bound to the felloe of one wheel, then the
other foot was bound to the felloe of the other
wheel.   The whole weight of the soldier was
thrown on his chest, which bore heavily against
the sharp edge of the rack.   It is almost un-
necessary to say that a gag was strapped into
the prisoner's mouth to prevent articulation,
before he was extended on the rack.   No man
could endure the supreme pain inflicted by this
torture without screaming.   I have seen a
strong and most determined man faint in less
than ten minutes under the strain of this severe
and brual punishment, to be cut down and
never again twirl sponge staff.   I have heard
men beg to be killed rather than to be tied on
the rack.

   To be bucked and gagged?   Yes, that was
severe, but not dangerous.   It was highly dis-
agreeable and painful, too, if prolonged, and at
all times calculated to make a man's eyes stick
out of his head as lobsters' eyes do.   And then
the appearance of a man while undergoing the
punishment was highly discreditable.   The soldier about to be bucked and gagged, generally
a drunken or noisy soldier, was forced to sit on
the ground ; his knees were drawn up to his

chin, then his hands were drawn forward to his shins, and there they were securely bound together. A long stick was then thrust under his knees and over his arms. A gag war then securely bound in his mouth. The soldier who was bucked and gagged could not hurt himself or any one else. He could not speak, but he could make inarticulate sounds indicative of his suffering, and he invariably made them before he was released.

Daily many men were tied up by the thumbs, and that was far from pleasant. The impudent bounty-jumper who had stood on his toes under a tree for a couple of hours to keep his weight off of his thumbs, which were tied to a limb over his head, was exceedingly apt to heed the words of his officers when next they spoke to him. The bounty-jumper lacked the moral qualities which could be appealed to in an honest endeavor to create a soldier out of a ruffian; but his capacity to suffer physically was unimpaired, and that had to be played upon.

Then there was the utterly useless and shoulder-chafing punishment of carrying a stick of cord-wood. The stick that one picked up so cheerfully, and stepped off with so briskly, and walked up and down before a sentinel with so gayly in the early morning, had an unaccountable property of growing heavier and heavier as the sun rose higher and higher. One morning at ten o'clock I dropped a stick that did not weigh more than twelve pounds at sunrise. I sat down by it and turned it over and over. It had not grown, but I was then willing to swear that it had gained one hundred and eighty-eight pounds in weight during the time I had carried it.

One evening in March an order which invested General U. S. Grant with the command of all the armies of the United States was read to us. That night we talked long and earnestly about our new general, and wondered what manner of a man he was. Old soldiers, who had seen many military reputations—reputations which had been made in subordinate commands or in distant regions occupied by inferior Confederate troops—melt before the battle-fire of the Army of Northern Virginia, and expose the incapacity of our generals, shrugged their shoulders carelessly, and said indifferently; " Well, let Grant try what he can accomplish with the Army of the Potomac. He cannot be worse than his predecessors; and, if he is a fighter, he can find all the fighting he wants.

We have never complained that Lee's men would not fight. Whatever faults they may have, cowardice is not one of them. We welcome Grant. He cannot be weaker or more inefficient than the generals who have wasted the lives of our comrades during the past three years." But Grant's name aroused no enthusiasm. The Army of the Potomac had passed the enthusiastic stage, and was patiently waiting to be led to victory or to final defeat.

The enlisted men thoroughly discussed Grant's military capacity. Magazines, illustrated papers, and newspapers, which contained accounts of his military achievements, were sent for, and were eagerly and attentively read. I have seen an artillery private quickly sketch the watercourses of the West in the sand with a pointed stick, and ridge up the earth with his hands to represent mountain chains, and then seize successive handfuls of earth and drop them in little piles to represent Forts Henry and Donelson, and Pittsburg Landing, Vicksburg, and Chattanooga. And then the enlisted men would gather around the sketch and take sides for and against Grant as the story of the battle was read aloud from a newspaper. These discussions were fruitless but combat-provoking, and frequently the wranglers adjourned to a secluded spot outside of the camp and fought it out with their fists. One thing about Grant's assuming command of the Army of the Potomac that no private I talked with liked, and I talked with hundreds, was the duality of command. Meade was retained in command of the Army of the Potomac, and all orders affecting the army came through him. Still Grant was with us, and in command of the Potomac army, as well as of all other armies. There was a division of responsibility in the division of authority which impressed the enlisted men unfavorably. It looked as though the generals were hedging against future mistakes and disasters.

With Grant came stricter discipline and re-cruits by the thousand. Throughout April there was great activity in all our camps along the Rapidan. The army was reorganized, and many generals were sent to Washington for orders, and we saw no more of them. Staff officers constantly rode to and fro. Inspector-generals were busy. There was a mysterious hum and bustle in all our camps. At all the railroad stations long trains of cars, filled with provisions and forage, were unloaded. White-capped wagons, loaded with hard bread and barrels of salted pork, rolled heavily into regimental and battery camps. We knew that battle was near.

On the evening of May 3d we fell in for dress parade. Up and down the immense camp we could see regiment after regiment, battery after battery, fall into line. The bugles rang out clearly in the soft spring air, distant drums beat, and trumpets blared. Then there was silence most profound. We listened attentively to the orders to march. To the right, to the left, in the distance before us, and far behind us, cheers arose. Battery after battery, regiment after regiment, cheered until the men were hoarse. My comrades did not cheer. They seemed to be profoundly impressed, but not in the least elated. The wonted silence of the evening was repeatedly broken by the resounding shouts of distant troops, who could not contain their joy that the season of inactivity was over, and the campaign, which we all hoped would be short and decisive, was opened. That night many unwonted fires burned, and we knew that the veteran troops were destroying the camp equipage which they did not intend to carry.

Jellet, the gunner of the piece I served on,

came to me that evening, and kindly looked
into my knapsack, and advised me as to what
to keep and what to throw away. He cut my
kit down to a change of underclothing, three
pairs of socks, a pair of spare shoes, three
plugs of navy tobacco, a rubber blanket, and a
pair of woollen blankets.

"Now, my lad, Jellet said, " do not pick up
any thing, excepting food and tobacco, while
you are on the march. Get hold of all the
food you can. Cut haversacks from dead men.
Steal them from infantrymen if you can. Let
your aim be to secure food and food and still
more food, and keep your eyes open for tobacco. Do not look at clothing or shoes or blankets. You can always draw those articles from
the quartermaster. Stick to your gun through
thick and thin. Do not straggle. Fill your
canteen at every stream we cross and wherever
you get a chance elsewhere. Never wash your
feet until the day's march is over. If you do,
they will surely blister." And here Jellet became highly impressive and shook his index
finger at me warningly and solemnly, " and,"
he said, " get hold of food, and hang on to it ;
you will need it."

The next morning we had our things packed

and our breakfast eaten by sunrise. Our useless plunder was piled up ; to each bundle was
fastened a tag, on which was the name of its
owner. The pile was turned over to the battery quartermaster, who said he would take
good care of the property. He did, too—such
good care that we never again saw a particle of
it. I wanted to burn the camp, but the old
soldiers who had fought under McClellan, and
Burnside, and Hooker, and Meade, and Pope,
scornfully snubbed me. They said : " Leave
things as they are " and they added, significantly : " We may want them before snow
flies."

III.

MARCHING TO THE BATTLE OF THE WILDERNESS.

A T dawn on May 4, 1864, General Grant's last campaign opened. The enlisted men of the battery I served with ate breakfast and struck their camp at Brandy Station before sunrise. It was a beautiful morning, cool and pleasant. The sun arose above an oak forest that stood to the east of us, and its rays caused thousands of distant rifle barrels and steel bayonets to glisten as fire points. In all directions troops were falling into line. The air resounded with the strains of martial music. Standards were unfurled and floated lazily in the light wind. Regiments fell into line on the plain before us. We could see officers sitting on their horses before them, as though making brief speeches to their soldiers, and then the banners would wave, and the lines face to the right into column of fours and march off; and then the sound of exultant cheering would float to us. Short trains of white-capped and dust-raising wagons rolled across the plain. The heavy-artillery regiment of Germans serving as infantry, which had been encamped to our left during the winter, fell into line. We light-artillery men laughed to see the burdens these sturdy men had on their backs. All of the enlisted men of that regiment had one knapsack strapped on their broad backs, and many of them had two. A sturdy, kindly race, the Germans, and tenacious in holding on to property; but in those days they were ignorant of the power of a southern sun, and of the mysterious quality it possesses to cause men to loathe personal property which they have to carry on their shoulders, and to cast it carelessly by the roadside. Jellet, the gunner of the piece I served on, joined me as I stood leaning against a cool gun, watching the Germans make ready for a campaign. He smiled, and said, significantly: " They will throw away those loads before they camp to-night." A word of command rang out in front of their regiment. They faced to the right and marched toward Ely's Ford of the Rapidan, and toward the Wilderness that lay beyond. " Boots and saddles!" was cheerily blown. The light-artillery men stood to their guns. The horses were harnessed and hitched in, the drivers mounted, and we moved off to take position in the column directly behind the heavily-laden Germans. We were in high spirits; indeed we were frisky, and walked along gayly. The men talked of the coming battle, and they sang songs about the soul of John Brown, alleged to be marching on, songs indicative of a desire to hang Jeff. Davis to a sour apple-tree. The Germans were, as usual, full of song and exceedingly noisy. I irritably expressed a wish that they would be quiet. Jellet sagely advised me, saying: "Wait; take it easy. I know the road we are to march on. There will be no singing in that regiment this afternoon." But Jellet, the dear old boy, was always advising impatient young men "to take it easy," "to wait a bit," and "don't fret," and, as there was nothing else to do, the young men invariably followed Jellet's advice.

We marched toward Ely's Ford pretty steadily for a couple of hours. As we drew near it, we saw that the troops were beginning to jam around its approaches. They were being massed quicker than they could cross.

We halted at a short distance from the ford and impatiently waited for our turn to cross. Once over the river we would be in column and in our proper place. I noticed that the Germans in our front were sitting on their knapsacks engaged in mopping their faces with red handkerchiefs. And I also noticed that as the sun swung higher and higher toward the zenith their songs retired within their hairy throats. I mentioned these, to me, interesting facts to Jellet, and he tapped his nose significantly with his index finger and said: " Wait a bit. We will lay in provisions from those fellows soon." And then he smiled as he laid down the military law designed to guide the conduct of light-artillery men on the march: " Get food, honestly if you can, but get it ; and ever remember that we cannot have too much of it in the battery."

A staff officer rode out of the apparently confused mass of men jammed around the ford, and galloped toward us. As he passed the German soldiers, they slowly arose and, resuming their back-breaking burdens, marched off. The staff officer rode to us, and told our captain to follow the Germans closely. This gold-laced youth of the staff had a look of importance on his face that made us all smile. His manner was as though he that morning, single-handed and before breakfast, had vanquished a couple of maiden-devouring dragons. We crossed the Rapidan on a pontoon bridge, and filled our canteens and drank deeply as we crossed. Then we marched over a narrow strip of valley land; then came a long, steep hill that led up to the comparatively level table-land of the Wilderness. This was the hill that caused the Germans to part with their personal property. Spare knapsacks, bursting with rich-ness, were cast aside near its base. Blankets, musical instruments, spare boots, and innumer-able articles of doubtful utility outcropped about half way up the hill. This float sharply indicated that the lead, when we discovered it, would be a rich one. Near the top of the hill we found many well-filled haversacks, and we picked up every one of them and hung them on the limbers and caissons and guns. The mine was rich, and we worked it thoroughly. Now we began to come on stragglers—men who had overloaded themselves, or who were soft and unfit to march in their gross condition. These men, with flushed faces and shirts open at the neck, gazed enviously at us as we light-

artillery men walked jauntily by. We felt it a
duty to tenderly inquire into the condition of
the health of these exhausted men, and did so
pleasantly; but they, the ill-conditioned per-
sons, resented our expressions of love and pity
as though they had been insulting remarks.

On the upland we marched briskly. I saw
no inhabitants in this region. They had fled
before our advance, abandoning their homes.
The soil was poor and thin, and the fields were
covered with last year's dead grass, and this
grass was burning as we passed by. I saw the
burning grass fire fences and sweep into the
woods; and I wondered, as tiny whirlwinds
formed and carried revolving columns of sparks
through the battery, if the caissons and limber
chests were spark-tight. As none of the men
seemed to be in the least alarmed at the near
presence of fire, I ceased to worry, willing to
take my chances if an explosion occurred. We
marched steadily until the old Chancellorsville
House was in sight. Many of the trees standing around us were bullet-scarred. We stood
idly in the road for some time, then went on
for a few hundred yards, and parked in a field
by the road, with the Germans in camp ahead
of us. Beyond them brigades of troops lay

restfully around their camp-fires.   Other troops marched by rapidly, and late into the night the belated men trod heavily past our camp.

During the day we had occasionally heard the faint report of distant rifles or the heavy, muffled report of a gun, and we suspected that our cavalry was feeling of Lee's men, who were intrenched near Mine Run, but whose pickets were all over the adjacent country.   All of the enlisted men hoped that they would get through the Wilderness—a rugged, broken area of upland that extends from the Rapidan River close to Spottsylvania—without fighting. The timber is dense and scrubby, and the whole region is cut up by a labyrinth of roads which lead to clearings of charcoal pits and there end.   Deep ravines, thickly clad with brush and trees, furrow the forest.   The Confederates knew the region thoroughly.   Many of their soldiers had worked in the region, which is a mineral one.   They knew where the roads led to, where the water was, where the natural line of defence was.   We knew nothing, excepting that the Army of the Potomac, under Hooker, had once encountered a direful disaster on the outskirts of this desolate region. On all sides I heard the murmur of the enlisted men as they expressed the hope that they would not have to fight in the Wilderness.

In the evening, after supper, I walked with a comrade to the spot where General Pleasanton had massed his guns and saved the army under Hooker from destruction, by checking the impetuous onslaught of Stonewall Jackson's Virginian infantry, fresh from the pleasures of the chase of the routed Eleventh Corps. We walked to and fro over the old battle-field, looking at bullet-scarred and canister-riven trees. The men who had fallen in that fierce fight had apparently been buried where they fell, and buried hastily. Many polished skulls lay on the ground. Leg bones, arm bones, and ribs could be found without trouble. Toes of shoes, and bits of faded, weather-worn uniforms, and occasionally a grinning, bony, fleshless face peered through the low mound that had been hastily thrown over these brave warriors. As we wandered to and .fro over the battle-ground, looking at the gleaming skulls and whitish bones, and examining the exposed clothing of the dead to see if they had been Union or Confederate soldiers, many infantrymen joined us. It grew dark, and we built a fire at which to light our pipes close to where we thought Jackson's men had formed for the charge, as the graves were thickest there, and then we talked of the battle of the preceding year. We sat on long, low mounds. The dead were all around us. Their eyeless skulls seemed to stare steadily at us. The smoke drifted to and fro among us. The trees swayed and sighed gently in the soft wind. One veteran told the story of the burning of some of the Union soldiers who were wounded during Hooker's fight around the Wilderness, as they lay helpless in the woods. It was a ghastly and awe-inspiring tale as he vividly told it to us as we sat among the dead. This man finished his story by saying shudderingly :

" This region," indicating the woods beyond us with a wave of his arm, " is an awful place to fight in. The utmost extent of vision is about one hundred yards. Artillery cannot be used effectively. The wounded are liable to be burned to death. I am willing to take my chances of getting killed, but I dread to have a leg broken and then to be burned slowly ; and these woods will surely be burned if we fight here. I hope we will get through this chapparal without fighting," and he took off his cap and meditatively rubbed the dust off of the red clover leaf which indicated the division and corps he belonged to. As we sat silently smoking and listening to the story, an infantry soldier who had, unobserved by us, been prying into the shallow grave he sat on with his bayonet, suddenly rolled a skull on the ground before us, and said in a deep, low voice: "That is what you are all coming to, and some of you will start toward it to-morrow." It was growing late, and this uncanny remark broke up the group, most of the men going to their regimental camps. A few of us still sat by the dying embers and smoked. As we talked we heard picket-firing, not brisk, but at short intervals the faint report of a rifle quickly answered. And we reasoned correctly that a Confederate skirmish line was in the woods, and that battle would be offered in the timber. The intelligent enlisted men of the Second Corps with whom I talked that night listened attentively to the firing, now rising, now sinking into silence, to again break out in another place. All of them said that Lee was going to face Grant in the Wilderness, and they based their opinion on the presence of a Confederate skirmish line in the woods. And all of them agreed that the advantages of position

were with Lee, and that his knowledge of the
region would enable him to face our greatly
superior army in point of numbers, with a fair
prospect of success.   But every infantry soldier
I talked with was resolute in his purpose to
fight desperately and aid to win a victory that
would end the war, if it was possible to win it.

In all our armies in the civil war there was
among the enlisted men, the volunteers, a system of gathering and distributing news that
beat the information we received from division
and corps head-quarters both in time and accuracy.   The system was paralleled by that of
the slaves who walked the plantations lying
within the Confederacy, o' nights.   These army
news-reporters who walked through the camps
at night to meet other soldiers and gather intelligence and discuss the campaign, were almost invariably Americans.   I cannot recall
ever having met, on these night ranges, men of
other nationality.   There was a burning desire
among these men to know how other commands
fared, and to gather accurate information, so as
to correctly judge of the battle's tide, the prog-
ress of the campaign, and the morale of the
army.   The enlisted men knew of defeats and
successes long before they were published in

general orders. The truth is that the privates of the army—the volunteers without bounty I mean—never believed a report that was published from head-quarters, unless it corresponded with the information the " camp-walkers " had gathered. It was surprising how quickly important news relative to a battle or the campaign spread throughout the army. The news was carried from camp-fire to camp-fire at night, and it was generally reliable and wonderfully full and accurate. Often as I sat by the camp-fire, talking with my comrades, I have seen shadowy forms hurrying rapidly through the woods, or along the roads, and I knew men who were hungry for authentic news were beating the camps and battle-line to obtain it. Frequently these figures would halt, and then, seeing our fire with men around it, they would issue forth from the woods and join us. They would sit down, fill their pipes, light them with glowing coals, and then, with their rifles lying across their knees, ask for the Second Corps news, inquire as to our losses, and whether we had gained or lost ground, and what Confederate command was opposed to us. They would anxiously inquire as to the truth of rumors of disaster which they might have heard during the day.   They would listen attentively to what we said, and it was a point of honor not to give false information to these men.   And then they would briefly tell the Fifth, or Sixth, or Ninth Corps news, and quickly disappear in the darkness.   I have often, after a day's service at the guns, walked three miles in the dark to verify a rumor that affected our safety. With no disrespect to these natural-born soldiers and most intelligent men do I record the seemingly incongruous truth, that it was necessary to closely watch army news-gatherers. One and all they would steal haversacks. They invariably combined predatory raids on other men's portable property with news-gathering.   To rob a soldier was to rob a man who might be killed next day, and would not need property.

It was past midnight when I crept under the caisson of my gun and pillowed my head on my knapsack.   The distant rifle-shots on the picket-line grew fainter and fainter, then were lost in the nearer noises of the camps, and I slept.

IV.

THE BATTLE OF THE WILDERNESS.

THE next morning I was awakened by a bugle call to find the battery I belonged to almost ready to march. I hurriedly toasted a bit of pork and ate it, and quickly chewed down a couple of hard tack, and drank deeply from my canteen, and was ready to march when the battery moved. It was a delightful morning. Almost all the infantry which had been camped around us the previous evening had disappeared. We struck into the road, passed the Chancellorsville House, turned to the right, and marched up a broad turnpike toward the Wilderness forest. After marching on this road for a short distance we turned to the left on an old dirt road, which led obliquely into the woods. The picket firing had increased in volume since the previous evening, and there was no longer any doubt that we were to fight in the Wilderness. The firing was a pretty brisk rattle, and steadily increasing in volume. About ten o'clock in the morning the soft spring air resounded with a fierce yell, the sound of which was instantly drowned by a roar of musketry, and we knew that the battle of the Wilderness had opened. The battery rolled heavily up the road into the woods for a short distance, when we were met by a staff officer, who ordered us out, saying:

" The battle has opened in dense timber. Artillery cannot be used. Go into park in the field just outside of the woods."

We turned the guns and marched back and went into park. Battery after battery joined us, some coming out of the woods and others up the road from the Chancellorsville House, until some hundred guns or more were parked in the field. We were then the reserve artillery.

Ambulances and wagons loaded with medical supplies galloped on the field, and a hospital was established behind our guns. Soon men, singly and in pairs or in groups of four or five, came limping slowly or walking briskly, with arms across their breasts and their hands clutched into their blouses, out of the woods. Some carried their rifles. Others had thrown them away. All of them were bloody. They slowly filtered through the immense artillery park and asked, with bloodless lips, to be directed to a hospital. Powder smoke hung high above the trees in thin clouds. The noise in the woods was terrific. The musketry was a steady roll, and high above it sounded the inspiring charging cheers and yells of the now thoroughly excited combatants. At intervals we could hear the loud report of Napoleon guns, and we thought that Battery K of the Fourth United States Artillery was in action. By eleven o'clock the wounded men were coming out of the woods in streams, and they had various tales to tell. Bloody men from the battle-line of the Fifth Corps trooped through our park supporting more severely wounded comrades. The battle, these men said, did not incline in our favor. They insisted that the Confederates were in force, and that they, having the advantage of position and knowledge of the region, had massed their soldiers for the attack and outnumbered us at the points of conflict. They described the Confederate fire as wonderfully accurate. One man who had a ghastly flesh wound across his forehead said : " The Confederates are shooting to kill this time. Few of their balls strike the trees higher than ten feet from the ground., Small trees are already falling, having been cut down by rifle balls. There is hardly a Union battery in action," he added, after an instant's pause.

By noon I was quite wild with curiosity, and, confident that the artillery would remain in park, I decided to go to the battle-line and see what was going on. I neglected to ask my captain for permission to leave the battery, because I feared he would not grant my request, and I did not want to disobey orders by going after he had refused me. I walked out of camp and up the road. The wounded men were becoming more and more numerous. I saw men, faint from loss of blood, sitting in the shade cast by trees. Other men were lying down. All were pale, and their faces expressed great suffering. As I walked I saw a dead man lying under a tree which stood by the roadside. He had been shot through the chest and had struggled to the rear ; then, becoming exhausted or choked with blood, he had lain down on a carpet of leaves and died. His pockets were turned inside out. A little farther on I met a sentinel standing by the roadside. Other sentinels paced to and fro in the woods on each side of the road, or stood leaning against trees, looking in the direction of the battle-line, which was far ahead of them in the woods. I stopped to talk to the guard posted on the road. He eyed me inquiringly, and answered my question as to what he was doing there, saying: " Sending stragglers back to the front.", Then he added, in an explanatory tone :

" No enlisted man can go past me to the rear unless he can show blood."

He turned to a private who was hastening down the road, and cried :

" Halt ! "

The soldier, who was going to the rear, paid no attention to the command. Instantly the sentinel's rifle was cocked, and it rose to his shoulder. He coolly covered the soldier, and sternly demanded that he show blood. The man had none to show. The cowardly soldier was ordered to return to his regiment, and, greatly disappointed, he turned back. Wounded men passed the guard without being halted. These guards seemed to be posted in the rear of the battle-lines for the express purpose of intercepting the flight of cowards. At the time, it struck me as a quaint idea to picket the rear of an army which was fighting a desperate battle.

I explained to the sentinel that I was a light-artillery man, and that I wanted to see the fight.

"Can I go past you?" I inquired.

"Yes," he replied, "you can go up. But you had better not go," he added. "You have no distinctive mark or badge on your dress to indicate the arm you belong to. If you go up, you may not be allowed to return, and then," he added, as he shrugged his shoulders indifferently, "you may get killed. But suit yourself."

So I went on. There was very heavy firing to the left of the road in a chaparral of brush and scrubby pines and oaks. There the musketry was a steady roar, and the cheers and yells of the fighters incessant. I left the road and walked through the woods toward the battle-ground, and met many wounded men who were coming out. They were bound for the rear and the hospitals. Then I came on a body of troops lying in reserve,—a second line of battle, I suppose. I heard the hum of bullets as they passed over the low trees. Then I noticed that small limbs of trees were falling in a feeble shower in advance of me. It was as though an army

of squirrels were at work cutting off nut and
pine cone-laden branches preparatory to lay-
ing in their winter's store of food. Then, par-
tially obscured by a cloud of powder smoke,
I saw a straggling line of men clad in blue.
They were not standing as if on parade, but
they were taking advantage of the cover afforded by trees, and they were firing rapidly.
Their line officers were standing behind them
or in line with them. The smoke drifted to
and fro, and there were many rifts in it. I
saw scores of wounded men. I saw many dead
soldiers lying on the ground, and I saw men
constantly falling on the battle-line. I could
not see the Confederates, and, as I had gone
to the front expressly to see a battle, I
pushed on, picking my way from protective
tree to protective tree, until I was about forty
yards from the battle-line. The uproar was
deafening; the bullets flew through the air
thickly. Now our line would move forward a
few yards, now fall back. I stood behind a
large oak tree, and peeped around its trunk.
I heard bullets "spat" into this tree, and I
suddenly realized that I was in danger. My
heart thumped wildly for a minute; then my
throat and mouth felt dry and queer. A dead

sergeant lay at my feet, with a hole in his forehead just above his left eye. Out of this wound bits of brain oozed, and slid on a bloody trail into his eye, and thence over his cheek to the ground. I leaned over the body to feel of it. It was still warm. He could not have been dead for over five minutes. As I stooped over the dead man, bullets swept past me, and I became angry at the danger I had foolishly gotten into. I unbuckled the dead man's cartridge belt, and strapped it around me, and then I picked up his rifle. I remember standing behind the large oak tree, and dropping the ramrod into the rifle to see if it was loaded. It was not. So I loaded it, and before I fairly understood what had taken place, I was in the rear rank of the battle-line, which had surged back on the crest of a battle billow, bareheaded, and greatly excited, and blazing away at an indistinct, smoke-and-tree-obscured line of men clad in gray and slouch-hatted. As I cooled off in the heat of the battle fire, I found that I was on the Fifth Corps' line, instead of on the Second Corps' line, where I wanted to be. I spoke to the men on either side of me, and they stared at me, a stranger, and briefly said that the regiment, the distinctive number of which I have long since forgotten, was near the left of the Fifth Corps, and that they had been fighting pretty steadily since about ten o'clock in the morning, but with poor success, as the Confederates had driven them back a little. The fire was rather hot, and the men were falling pretty fast. Still it was not anywhere near as bloody as I had expected a battle to be. As a grand, inspiring spectacle, it was highly unsatisfactory, owing to the powder smoke obscuring the vision. At times we could not see the Confederate line, but that made no difference; we kept on firing just as though they were in full view. We gained ground at times, and then dead Confederates lay on the ground as thickly as dead Union soldiers did behind us. Then we would fall back, fighting stubbornly, but steadily giving ground, until the dead were all clad in blue.

Between two and three o'clock the fire in our front slackened. We did not advance. Indeed I saw no general officer on the battle-line to take advantage of any opportunity that the battle's tide might expose to a man of military talent. I had seen some general officers near the reserves, but none on the front line. I noticed the lack of artillery and saw that the nature of the ground forbade its use.   Our line was fed with fresh troops and greatly strengthened.   Boxes of cartridges were carried to us, and we helped ourselves.   We were standing behind trees or lying on the ground, and occasionally shooting at the Confederate line, or where their line should have been. Some of the old soldiers muttered about things in general, and rebel dodges in particular, and darkly hinted that the sudden slackening of the fire in our front boded no good to us. Soon a storm of yells, followed instantly by a roar of musketry, rolled to us from the left, and not distant.   Almost instantly it was followed by a cheer and a volley of musketry. We sprang to our feet and were in line, but there was nothing in strength ahead of us. To the left the noise increased in volume. The musketry was thunderous.   Soon affrighted men rushed through the woods to our rear, not in ones and twos, but in dozens and scores, and as they swept past us they cried loudly :

    " We are flanked ! ᐧ Hill's corps has got around our left."

    Officers gave commands which I did not understand, but I did as my comrades did, and we were speedily placed at right angles to our original position, which was held by a heavy skirmish line. Many of the men who were running from the battle-field dropped into our line and remained with us until nightfall. I saw men from a dozen different regiments standing in our line. We were dreadfully nervous, and felt around blindly for a few minutes, not knowing what to do. Then we were reassured by seeing a staff officer explaining something to the commander of the regiment, a young major. This officer passed the word along the line that the Second Corps had come up just in time to close up a gap between the two corps, through which the Confederate general, Hill, had endeavored to thrust a heavy column of infantry. Speedily we got back into our original position. In a few minutes we saw a thin line of gray figures, not much heavier than a strong skirmish line, advancing rapidly toward us. They yelled loudly and continuously. We began firing rapidly, and so did they. They came quite close to us, say within seventy-five yards, and covered themselves as well as they could. We could see them fairly well, and shot many of them, and they killed and wounded many Union soldiers. Soon we drove them to cover, and they were comparatively quiet. The noise to the left, where Hancock's corps was fighting, almost drowned the racket we were making. The Confederate charge against the portion of the Fifth Corps where I was fighting was not delivered with vim. It impressed me as a sham. Their line, as I said, was thin, and it lacked momentum. I spoke to my fellows about it, and they all agreed that it was not earnest fighting, but a sham to cover the real attack on our left. There the battle raged with inconceivable fury for about two hours. Then the fight died down, and excepting for picket-firing, the lines were silent.

The wounded soldiers lay scattered among the trees. They moaned piteously. The unwounded troops, exhausted with battle, helped their stricken comrades to the rear. The wounded were haunted with the dread of fire. They conjured the scenes of the previous year, when some wounded men were burned to death, and their hearts well-nigh ceased to beat when they thought they detected the smell of burning wood in the air. The bare prospect of fire running through the woods where they lay helpless, unnerved the most courageous of men, and made them call aloud for help. I saw many wounded soldiers in the Wilderness who hung on to their rifles, and whose intention was clearly stamped on their pallid faces. I saw one man, both of whose legs were broken, lying on the ground with his cocked rifle by his side and his ramrod in his hand, and his eyes set on the front. I knew he meant to kill himself in case of fire—knew it as surely as though I could read his thoughts. The dead men lay where they fell. Their haversacks and cartridges had been taken from their bodies. The battle-field ghouls had rifled their pockets. I saw no dead man that night whose pockets had not been turned inside out.

Soon after dark the story of the fight on our left had been gathered by the newsmongers, and we learned that the Second Corps had saved itself from rout and the army from defeat by the most dogged fighting, and that they had required the aid of Getty's division of the Sixth Corps to enable them to hold their own. That news was sufficient to start me. So I went down the line, walking through the woods, stumbling over the dead and being cursed by the living, until I came to the Second Corps. There I found a regiment, the Fortieth New York, if I correctly recall the number, some of whose soldiers I knew.   They told me the story of the fight.   It was really told by the windrows of dead men, and the loud and continuous shrieks and groans of the wounded. I was still bareheaded, and I fitted myself with a hat from a collection of hats lying near some dead men.   And I took a pair of blankets from the shoulders of a dead man and slept in them that night.

Early the next morning, long before sunrise, I had my breakfast, and having seen sufficient of the fighting done by infantry, and strongly impressed with the truth that a light-artillery man had better stay close to his guns, I bade my acquaintances good-by, and walked off, intent on getting to my gun and comparative comfort and safety.   But I hung on to my rifle and belt.   They were to be trophies of the battle, and I meant to excite the envy of my comrades by displaying them.   Stepping into the road I walked along briskly, and saw many other unwounded men rearward bound.   A sentinel, with rifle at the carry, halted me, and demanded to see blood.   I could show none. I assured him that I belonged to the light artillery, and that I had gone to the front the previous day just to see the battle.

He said : " You have a rifle ; you have a belt and a cartridge box. Your mouth is powder-blackened. You have been fighting as an infantryman, and you shall so continue to fight. You go back, or I will arrest you, and then you will be sent back."

To say that I was amazed and disgusted would but faintly express my feelings. There stood the provost guard, who would not let me go home to my battery. I longed to kill him —longed to show the Army of the Potomac one dead provost guard ; but I was afraid to shoot him, for fear that his comrades might see me do it. So I turned and hastened back to the front. I determined to fight that day, and go home to the battery the, succeeding night. I did not believe that the line of guards extended far into the woods, and even if they did I knew that I could pass through the lines in the night. Before I rejoined the infantry who were on the battle-line I equipped myself with a plug of tobacco and two canteens filled with water—never mind where I got them.

Away off to the right, toward the Rapidan, the battle rose with the sun. In our front, the Second Corps, there was little movement discernible. But so dense was the cover that we could see but little at a distance of two hundred yards. I saw that the soldiers had thrown up a slight intrenchment during the previous night. About five o'clock we were ordered to advance, and pushed ahead, fighting as we went, and forced Hill's men back, killing many, wounding more, and taking scores of prisoners. We crossed a road, which a wounded Confederate told me was the Brock road. I saw many dead Confederates during this advance. They were poorly clad. Their blankets were in rolls, hanging diagonally from the left shoulder to the right side, where the ends were tied with a string or a strap. Their canvas haversacks contained plenty of corn-meal and some bacon. I saw no coffee, no sugar, no hard bread in any of the Confederate haversacks I looked into. But there was tobacco in plugs on almost all the dead Confederates. Their arms were not as good as ours. They were poorly shod. The direful poverty of the Confederacy was plainly indicated by its dead soldiers. But they fought? Yes, like men of purely American blood. We had charged, and charged, and charged again, and had gone wild with battle fever. We had gained about two miles of ground. We were doing splendidly. I cast my eyes upward to see the sun, so as to judge of the time, as I was hungry and wanted to eat, and I saw that it was still low above the trees. The Confederates seemed to be fighting more stubbornly, fighting as though their battle-line was being fed with more troops. They hung on to the ground they occupied tenaciously, and resolutely refused to fall back further. Then came a swish of bullets and a fierce exultant yell, as of thousands of infuriated tigers. Our men fell by scores. Great gaps were struck in our lines. There was a lull for an instant, and then Longstreet's men sprang to the charge. It was swiftly and bravely made, and was within an ace of being successful. There was great confusion in our line. The men wavered badly. They fired wildly. They hesitated. I feared the line would break; feared that we were whipped. The line was fed with troops from the reserve. The regimental officers held their men as well as they could. We could hear them close behind us, or in line with us, saying : " Steady, men, steady, steady, steady ! " as one speaks to frightened and excited horses. The Confederate fire resembled the fury of hell in intensity, and was deadly accurate. Their bullets swished by in swarms. It seems to me that I could have caught a pot full of them if I had had a strong iron vessel rigged on a pole as a butterfly net. Again our line became wavy and badly confused, and it was rapidly being shot into a skirmish-like order of formation. Speedily a portion of the Ninth Corps came to our assistance, and they came none too soon. They steadied the line and we regained heart. During this critical time, when the fate of the Second Corps was trembling in the balance, many officers rushed to and fro behind us, but I saw no major-generals among them ; but then I had sufficient to do to look ahead and fall back without falling down, and they may have been on the battle-line, only I did not see them. The Confederates got a couple of batteries into action, and they added to the deafening din. The shot and shell from these guns cut great limbs off of the trees, and these occasionally fell near the battle-line, and several men were knocked down by them. Our line strengthened, we, in our turn, pushed ahead, and Longstreet's men gave ground slowly before us, fighting savagely for every foot. The wounded lay together. I saw, in the heat of this fight, wounded men of the opposing forces aiding each other to reach the protective shelter of trees and logs, and, as we advanced, I saw a Confederate and a Union soldier drinking in turn out of a Union canteen, as they lay behind a tree.

There was another lull, and then the charging line of gray again rushed to the assault with inconceivable fury. We fired and fired and fired, and fell back fighting stubbornly. We tore cartridges until our teeth ached. But we could not check the Confederate advance, and they forced us back and back and back until we were behind the slight intrenchments along the Brock road. A better charge, or a more determined, I never saw. We fought savagely at the earthworks. At some points the timber used in the earthworks was fired, and our men had to stand back out of the line of flame and shoot through it at the Confederates, who were fighting in front of the works. And the woods, through which we had fallen back, were set on fire, and many wounded soldiers were burned to death. We beat off the Confederates, and they, with the exception of the picket line, disappeared. Our line was straightened, reserves were brought up, and some of the battle-torn troops were relieved. We had half an hour's rest, during which time many of us

ate and smoked, and drank out of our canteens;
and we talked, though not so hopefully as in the
early morning.   Men missed old comrades, and
with only seeming indifference figuratively
reckoned they had "turned up their toes."
Firing had almost ceased.   It was as the cessation of the wind before the approach of a
cyclone.   A tempest of fire and balls and yells
broke out on the right.   We were out of it.
The real battle raged furiously in the woods to
the right, while a heavy line of Confederate
skirmishers, who lurked skilfully behind trees
and who fired briskly and accurately, made
things decidedly unpleasant for us, and effectu-
ally prevented any men being drawn from our
portion of the line to strengthen the right.
How we fretted while this unseen combat
raged!   We judged that our men were being
worsted as the battle-sounds passed steadily to
our rear.   Then the fugitives, the men quick
to take alarm and speedy of foot when faced
to the rear, began to pass diagonally through
the woods behind us.   While we stood quiver-
ing with nervous excitement, and gazing anxiously into each other's eyes, we heard a solid
roll of musketry, as though a division had fired
together, cheers followed, and then the battle-

sound rapidly advanced toward the Confederate line. Then all was quiet, and the fighting on the left of our line was over. Soon word was passed along the line that the charging Confederates had broken through the left of the Ninth Corps, and would have cut the army in twain if General Carroll had not caught them on the flank and driven them back with the Third Brigade of the Second Division of the Second Corps.

The enlisted men supposed the day's fighting was over. And so did our generals. But the Confederates marched swiftly on many parallel roads, and were massed for an attack on our right, the Sixth Corps. They were skilfully launched and ably led, and they struck with terrific violence against Shaler's and Seymour's brigades, which were routed, with a loss of 4,000 prisoners. The Confederates came within an ace of routing the Sixth Corps; but the commanders restored and steadied the lines, and the Confederate charge was first checked and then bloodily repulsed.

The day's offensive fighting on the part of the Confederates, as we, the enlisted men, summed it up, had consisted of two general assaults delivered all along our line, as though to feel of us and discover where we were the weakest, and to promptly take advantage of the knowledge gained, to attack in force and with surprising vim and stanchness first one flank and then the other.   Both of the assaults were dangerously near being successful.

The sun sank, and the gloom among the trees thickened and thickened until darkness reigned in the forest where thousands of dead and wounded men lay.   The air still smelled of powder-smoke.   Many soldiers cleaned out their rifles.   We ate, and then large details helped to carry their wounded comrades to the road, where we loaded them into ambulances and wagons.   I determined to join my battery. I threw away my rifle and belt, and as the first wagons loaded with wounded men moved to the rear, I walked by the side of the column and passed the guards, if there were any stationed on that road, without being challenged. When I was well to the rear, I for the first and last time became a " coffee boiler."   I cooked and ate a hearty supper, and then rolled myself in the dead soldier's blankets, which I had hung on to, and slept soundly until morning, when I found the battery I belonged to without much trouble, and was promptly punished for being absent without leave.

About ten o'clock in the morning I was sitting by the battery wagon, sullenly nursing my sore arms and shoulders and my wrath. I had had an experience of packing a stick of wood on my shoulder in front of a guard, who skilfully touched me up with the point of his sabre when I lagged, that had soured my usually sweet temper. And I was ill-tempered when wounded men began to drift through the guns. The noise in the woods had sunk to skirmish-firing. The wounded men said that the third day's fighting opened with a little artillery practice at nothing, which was not answered, and that then the men who carried rifles investigated matters, and promptly discovered that the Confederates had intrenched themselves during the night.

That evening the troops began to pour out of the woods in columns. The infantry soldiers marched soberly past the artillery. There were no exultant songs in those columns. The men seemed aged. They were very tired and very hungry. They seemed to be greatly depressed. I sat by the roadside, in front of the battery, waiting for it to move, and attentively watched the infantry march past. Many of the soldiers spoke to me, asking if there was authentic news as to where they were going. Some of these men were slightly wounded. I noticed that the wounded men who stuck to their colors were either Irish or Americans, and that they had the stride and bearing of veterans. There was a gap in the column, and my battery moved on to the road, and other batteries followed us. We marched rapidly and without halting, until we reached a point where another road, which led in the direction of the right of our battle-line, joined the road we were on. Here we met a heavy column of troops marching to the rear, as we were. The enlisted men were grave, and rather low in spirits, and decidedly rough in temper. Marching by my side was a Vermont Yankee sergeant whose right cheek had been slightly burnt by a rifle-ball, not enough to send him to the rear, but sufficient to make him irritable and ill-tempered. He talked bitterly of the fight. His men talked worse. They one and all asserted that the army was not whipped, that they had not been properly handled in the two first days' fighting, and that the two days' fighting had resulted in a Confederate loss almost, if not quite, equal to ours, as the fighting was generally outside of the earthworks.

"Here we go," said a Yankee private; "here we go, marching for the Rapidan, and the protection afforded by that river. Now, when we get to the Chancellorsville House, if we turn to the left, we are whipped—at least so say Grant and Meade. And if we turn toward the river, the bounty-jumpers will break and run, and there will be a panic."

"Suppose we turn to the right, what then?" I asked.

"That will mean fighting, and fighting on the line the Confederates have selected and intrenched. But it will indicate the purpose of Grant to fight," he replied.

Then he told me that the news in his Sixth Corps brigade was that Meade had strongly advised Grant to turn back and recross the Rapidan, and that this advice was inspired by the loss of Shaler's and Seymour's brigades on the evening of the previous day. This was the first time I heard this rumor, but I heard it fifty times before I slept that night. The enlisted men, one and all, believed it, and I then believed the rumor to be authentic, and I believe it to-day. None of the enlisted men had any confidence in Meade as a tenacious, aggressive fighter. They had seen him allow the

Confederates to escape destruction after Gettysburg, and many of them openly ridiculed him and his alleged military ability.

Grant's military standing with the enlisted men this day hung on the direction we turned at the Chancellorsville House. If to the left, he was to be rated with Meade and Hooker and Burnside and Pope—the generals who preceded him. At the Chancellorsville House we turned to the right. Instantly all of us heard a sigh of relief. Our spirits rose. We marched free. The men began to sing. The enlisted men understood the flanking movement. That night we were happy. There was much interchange of opinion between the artillerymen and the infantry. We gathered from the losses these men enumerated in their own commands that the three days' fighting had cost Grant about twenty-five thousand men, or a little more than one fifth of the army. And the enlisted men—the volunteers who had brains in their skulls—always insisted that those figures correctly represented the losses of Union soldiers in the bloody Wilderness battle.

V.

FIGHTING AROUND SPOTTSYLVANIA.

MAY 8, 1864. The bloody battle of the
Wilderness was a thing of the past.
That dense chaparral in which the unburied
dead Union and Confederate soldiers lay scattered thickly was being left behind us as we
marched. In the morning the guns of the
Fifth Corps notified the Union troops that the
Confederates had been found. The Fifth
Corps had been in the advance in the flank
movement to the left out of the Wilderness,
and Longstreet's corps had marched parallel
with it, and had taken position behind the
river Ny, which was more properly a creek.
We were not in this fight, but correctly judged
that it was not severe, as at no time did the
battle's roar rise to the volume which indicates
a fierce engagement. On May 9th the army
was clear of the Wilderness. We took position
around Spottsylvania Court-House. Wherever
we went there were heavy earthworks, behind

which the veteran Confederate infantry lurked. The day was spent in getting into position and in bloody wrangling between the opposing pickets and in sharpshooting. At intervals would be a crash of musketry and a cheer; then the artillery would open and fire briskly for a few minutes. But there was no real fighting. That night we heard that General Sedgwick, commanding the Sixth Corps, had been killed by a sharpshooter or by a stray ball from the Confederate picket line.

May 10th, and the fighting began. The din of the battle was continuous, and as much of the artillery had been drawn to the battle-line the noise was far louder than it had been in the Wilderness. The troops fought all day. A solid roll of musketry, mingled with the thunderous reports of cannon quickly served, caused the air to quiver. After fighting all day, we spent a large portion of the night in fruitless endeavors to flank the Confederate position. Spent it in following staff officers, to find that we were again in front of earthworks, which were lined with keen-eyed, resolute infantry soldiers. In Spottsylvania we fought by day, we marched by night, and our losses were exceedingly large.

One day the battery I served with was parked for rest near a road down which wounded men were streaming in a straggling column. These men, tired, weakened by loss of blood, and discouraged, tumbled exhausted into the angles of worm fences, and spread their blankets from rail to rail to make a shade. There they rested and patiently waited for their turn at the surgeons' tables. They were a ghastly array. The sight of these poor, stricken men as they helped one another, as they bound one another's wounds, as they painfully hobbled to and fro for water, was a most pathetic one. They lined the roadside for half a mile, a double hedgerow of suffering and death, as men were dying in the fence corners every few minutes. Down the road we heard the stirring music of a martial band. Soon the head of a column of troops came in sight. Officers were riding at the head of the soldiers on horses that pranced. The men were neatly clad, and their brass shoulder-plates shone brightly in the sun.

" The heavy-artillery men from the fortifications around Washington," one of my comrades murmured.

These fresh soldiers were marching beautifully. They were singing loudly and tunefully.

They were apparently pleased with the prospect of fighting in defence of their country. For some reason the infantry of the line—the volunteer infantry—did not admire heavy-artillery men. They liked light-artillery men, and were encouraged by the presence of the guns on the battle-line. There was something inspiring in the work of the gunners and in the noisy reports of the cannon; and, then, cannon were deadly, and if well served and accurately aimed, they could and did pulverize charging columns. But heavy-artillery men were soldiers of a different breed. There was a widespread belief among us that these men had enlisted in that arm because they expected to fight behind earthworks, or to safely garrison the forts which surrounded Washington. We did not like these troops. The head of the heavy-artillery column, the men armed as infantry, was thrust among the wounded who lined the roadside. These bloody wrecks of soldiers derided the new-comers. Men would tauntingly point to a shattered arm, or a wounded leg, or to bloody wounds on their faces, or to dead men lying in fence corners, and derisively shout: " That is what you will catch up yonder in the woods ! " and they would solemnly indicate the

portion of the forest they meant by extending
arms from which blood trickled in drops. I
saw one group of these wounded men repeatedly cover and uncover with a blanket a dead
man whose face was horribly distorted, and
show the courage-sapping spectacle to the
marching troops, and faintly chuckle and cause
their pale cheeks to bulge with derisive tongue-
thrusts, as they saw the heavy-artillery men's
faces blanch. Still others would inquire in
mock solicitous tones as to the locality of
their cannon, and then tenderly 'inquire of
some soldier whose bearing or dress caught
their attention; " Why, dearest, why did you
leave your earthwork behind you?" And they
would hobble along and solemnly assure the man
that he had made a serious mistake, and that
he should have brought the earthwork along,
as he would need it in yonder woods, pointing
with outstretched bloody arms to the forest,
where the battle's roar resounded. Others as-
sumed attitudes of mock admiration and gazed
impudently and contemptuously at the full regiments as they marched by. Long before the
heavy-artillery men had passed through the
bloody gauntlet their songs were hushed.
They became grave and sober-minded. For

the first time they realized what war meant. It was not play. It was not pleasure. It was not sport under the greenwood trees, but a savage encounter with desperate adversaries, who dealt death and grievous wounds with impartial hands. These troops passed us and entered the woods and the battle, and I am proud to say that their fighting was superb. They fought with a steadiness and determination that could not be excelled. The whole army honored them. After Spottsylvania I never heard a word spoken against the heavy-artillery men whom Grant summoned from Washington to make good his losses in the Wilderness.

The movable fight dragged along until May 12th. We fought here. We charged there. We accomplished nothing. But early on the morning of May 12th the Second Corps carried by assault the Confederate works held by Johnston's division of Ewell's corps, capturing about three thousand five hundred prisoners and thirty guns. Our troops caught the battle-exhausted Confederates asleep in their blankets. The Confederate line was broken. Their army was cut in twain. But it amounted to nothing. If the advantage had been intelligently followed up, it might have had decisive results. As it was, many thousands of enlisted men were killed and wounded in a furious fight which lasted all day, and the next morning we found that the Confederates had fortified a line in rear of the captured works, and our losses of thousands of brave men resulted in nothing but the capture of twenty guns (ten of these guns which were captured by the Second Corps were wrested from them by Ewell's men in the fights that ensued).

That night a wounded Second Corps soldier came into our battery, and joined me at the fire. He asked for food. I had plenty, and as the man's right arm was stiff from a wound, I told him I would cook a supper for him if he would wait. He greedily accepted the invitation. Soon I had a mess of pork and hardtack frying and coffee boiling, and as I had that day found a haversack—truth is that its owner, a heavy-artillery man, was asleep when I found it —which contained a can of condensed milk and half a loaf of light bread, the wounded soldier and I had a feast. After supper we smoked and talked. He told, in vivid, descriptive language, of the day's fighting, of the capture of the guns, and of the strength of the Confederate intrenchments. Soberly he said·

" The Army of the Potomac has always longed for a fighting general—one who would fight, and fight, and fight,—and now it has got him. But," he added, " he does not seem to know that Lee's veteran infantry cannot be driven out of skilfully constructed earthworks by direct assault. I am afraid he will waste the army by dashing it against works that cannot be captured. The enlisted men have been sacrificed to-day," he added sadly, " and unlike the results in the Wilderness fight, we have killed but few Confederates, except at the captured forts."

This was the first complaint I heard against Grant. I heard plenty before the campaign closed.

" The Wilderness," said my wounded guest, " was a private's battle. The men fought as best they could, and fought stanchly. The generals could not see the ground, and if they were on the front line, they could not have seen their troops. The enlisted men did not expect much generalship to be shown. All they expected was to have the battle-torn portions of the line fed with fresh troops. There was no chance for a display of military talent on our side, only for the enlisted men to fight,

and fight, and fight; and that they did cheerfully and bravely. Here the Confederates are
strongly intrenched, and it was the duty of
our generals to know the strength of the
works (we all knew the dogged fighting capacity of their defenders) before they launched
the army against them." The intelligent
private's criticism of the military capacity of
our generals struck me as eminently correct,
and made me thoughtful. My guest was
tired, and first exacting a promise from me
that I would give him his breakfast, he lay on
his back behind a tree, and after I had bathed
his wounded arm he slept.

We marched to and fro. The infantry were
almost constantly engaged in feeling of the
Confederate lines to find a weak place, and
finding all points stanchly defended. The
artillery was pleasantly employed in burying
good iron in Confederate earthworks. The
list of our killed and wounded and missing
grew steadily and rapidly, longer and longer,
as their cartridge-boxes grew lighter and lighter. One day a brisk fight was going on in
front of us. We were ordered to the top of
a hill and told to fire over our infantry into the
edge of the woods, where the Confederates lay.

The battery swung into action. Below us, in the open, was a pasture field. In it were two batteries and a line of infantry. The former were noisily engaged; the latter were not doing much of any thing. The Confederates were behind an earthwork that stood, shadowed by trees, in the edge of the forest, and it was evident that they meant to stay there. Our infantry charged, and at some points they entered the edge of the woods, out of which they speedily came, followed by a disorderly and heavy line of Confederate skirmishers. The batteries in the open were skilfully handled and admirably served, but it was a matter of a very short time for them. As soon as our infantry got out of range in a ravine, the Confederate skirmishers dropped prone on the ground, disappeared behind trees, sank into holes, squatted behind bushes, and turned their attention to the Union batteries, which were within rifle range of the skirmishers, and the guns were almost instantly driven from the field, leaving many horses, and men clad in blue, lying on the ground. Then the Confederate skirmishers ran back to their earthworks and clambered over. The battery I served with was firing three-inch percussion bolts at the Confederate line and doing no harm. One of my comrades spoke to me across the gun, saying: "Grant and Meade are over there," nodding his head to indicate the direction in which I was to look. I turned my head and saw Grant and Meade sitting on the ground under a large tree. Both of them were watching the fight which was going on in the pasture field. Occasionally they turned their glasses to the distant wood, above which small clouds of white smoke marked the bursting shells and the extent of the battle. Across the woods that lay behind the pasture, and behind the bare ridge that formed the horizon, and well within the Confederate lines, a dense column of dust arose, its head slowly moving to our left. I saw Meade call Grant's attention to this dust column, which was raised either by a column of Confederate infantry or by a wagon train. We ceased firing, and sat on the ground around the guns watching our general, and the preparations that were being made for another charge. Grant had a cigar in his mouth. His face was immovable and expressionless. His eyes lacked lustre. He sat quietly and watched the scene as though he was an uninterested spectator. Meade was nervous, and his hand constantly sought his face, which it stroked. Staff officers rode furiously up and down the hill carrying orders and information. The infantry below us in the ravine formed for another charge. Then they started on the run for the Confederate earthworks, cheering loudly the while. We sprang to our guns and began firing rapidly over their heads at the edge of the woods. It was a fine display of accurate artillery practice, but, as the Confederates lay behind thick earthworks, and were veterans not to be shaken by shelling the outside of a dirt bank behind which they lay secure, the fire resulted in emptying our limber chests, and in the remarkable discovery that three-inch percussion shells could not be relied upon to perform the work of a steam shovel. Our infantry advanced swiftly, but not with the vim they had displayed a week previous; and when they got within close rifle range of the works, they were struck by a storm of rifle-balls and canister that smashed the front line to flinders. They broke for cover, leaving the ground thickly strewed with dead and dying men. The second line of battle did not attempt to make an assault, but returned to the ravine. Grant's face never changed its expression. He sat impassive and smoked steadily, and watched the short-lived battle and decided defeat without displaying emotion. Meade betrayed great anxiety. The fight over, the generals arose and walked back to their horses, mounted and rode briskly away, followed by their staff. No troops cheered them. None evinced the slightest enthusiasm. The enlisted men looked curiously at Grant, and after he had disappeared they talked of him, and of the dead and wounded men who lay in the pasture field; and all of them said just what they thought, as was the wont of American volunteers. This was the only time that I saw either Grant or Meade under fire during the campaign, and then they were within range of rifled cannon only.

Toward evening of the eighth day's fighting a furious attack was made on our right by Ewell's corps. This attack was repulsed, and then the battle died down to picket-firing and sharpshooting. Now and then a battery would fire a few shot into a Confederate earthwork, just to let its defenders know that we still lived. We were strongly intrenched, and it was evident to the enlisted men that the battles fought around Spottsylvania belonged to the past.

We estimated our losses up to this time at from forty-five thousand to fifty thousand men, or about two fifths of the men whom Grant took across the Rapidan. I slept from 6 P.M. of the eighth day's fighting until 2 P.M. of the ninth day's fighting. I made up the losses of sleep incurred during the eight days and nights of almost continuous fighting and marching. This sleep was so profound that I barely heard the guns as they occasionally roared over my head. I was easy in my mind, as I knew that some hollow-eyed comrade would awaken me if I was needed at the guns or if we moved.

I breakfasted about 3 P.M., and then, feeling frisky, volunteered to go to a spring a quarter of a mile to the rear, the first portion of the path to which was commanded by Confederate rifles. The crew of the gun I belonged to loaded me down with their empty canteens, and I ran, to avoid the sharpshooter's fire, to the protection of the forest behind us. There I saw many soldiers. Hollow-eyed, tired-looking men they were, too, but not " coffee-boilers," lying on the ground sleeping soundly. They had sought the comparative safety of the forest to sleep. Near the spring, which rose in a dense thicket through which a spring run flowed, the shade was thick and the forest gloomy. The water in the spring had been roiled, so I searched for another higher up the run. While searching for it I saw a colonel of infantry put on his war paint. It was a howling farce in one act—one brief act of not more than twenty seconds' duration, but the fun of the world was crowded into it. This blond, bewhiskered brave sat safely behind a large oak tree. He looked around quickly. His face hardened with resolution. He took a cartridge out of his vest pocket, tore the paper with his strong white teeth, spilled the powder into his right palm, spat on it, and then, first casting a quick glance around to see if he was observed, he rubbed the moistened powder on his face and hands, and then dust-coated the war paint. Instantly he was transformed from a trembling coward who lurked behind a tree into an exhausted brave taking a little well-earned repose. I laughed silently at the spectacle, and filled my canteens at a spring I found, and then rejoined my comrades, and together we laughed at and then drank to the health of the blonde warrior. That night I slept and dreamed of comic plays and extravagant burlesques; but in the wildest of dream vagaries there was no picture that at all compared with the actual one I had seen in the forest. That colonel is yet alive. I saw him two years ago.

VI.

THE FLANK MOVEMENT FROM SPOTTSYLVANIA TO THE NORTH ANNA RIVER.

FOR fifteen days we had been fighting in the Wilderness and at Spottsylvania, and it was with great joy that the enlisted men of the Second Corps received on the afternoon of May 20, 1864, the order to withdraw from our foul intrenchments and march to the rear. Other troops occupied our earthworks as we marched out. Our officers assured us that we were to have a rest. We needed it. Fifteen days of battle—fifteen days of continuous and bloody fighting—had exhausted us physically, and had unstrung our nerves. We fell back to a piece of woods, and prepared to enjoy a night's unbroken sleep. The guns were parked. The picket rope was stretched, and some horses were tied to it, when a head-quarter's orderly rode briskly into our camp and delivered an order to our captain. The enlisted men ceased their preparations for making a night of it, and watched the orderly. The captain read the order, receipted for it and then ordered the chests of the gun limbers to be filled with ammunition, and supplemented that with another, commanding the chief of caissons to take them to the rear to the ammunition train and fill them. The enlisted men did not relish these orders. They sharply indicated that we were not to have a long, unbroken sleep. In a few minutes the battery quartermaster came into camp, accompanied by his wagons, which were loaded with forage and rations. The line sergeants loudly called: "Fall in for rations!" and the gun detachments marched to the wagons, where six days' rations were issued to us. Sacks of grain were thrown on the ground, preparatory to being loaded on the limbers and caissons. To the right, to the left of us, heavy six-mule teams rolled into the infantry camps, and the soldiers gathered around them with open haversacks, which were speedily filled. Men who were bathing at a run which flowed near us, or who were seated shirt in hand on the ground, endeavoring to pick the vermin off of that garment, put on their clothing and hurried to the wagons. Then other wagons, which chucked heavily into ruts, rolled into the infantry camps, and chests filled with ammunition were thrown out and ripped open, and the soldiers helped themselves. Cartridge-boxes were filled until they sagged heavily on the supporting belts.

After eating an early supper I walked over to the nearest infantry regiment, and found most of the men lying on the ground, sleeping soundly by their stacked muskets. A few groups of earnest, intelligent soldiers sat under trees studying the war maps of Virginia which were open before them. These men told me that six days' rations—and generous rations, too—had been issued to them, and that every enlisted man had forty rounds of ammunition in his cartridge-box and twenty in his pockets. I sat with these men for an hour. We talked of the campaign, and studied the maps, and finally concluded that the Second Corps was to march that night to our left, and attempt to get around the Confederate right. Not a man of the group I was with believed that the movement would be successful. We knew, and the maps showed, that the Confederates had the shortest line to march on, and we had heard from cavalry privates who had ridden south on raids or who had operated on the flanks of the army, that the important strategic points and natural lines of defence that lay in the region intervening between us and Richmond had all been carefully fortified. But whether the movement would be successful or not, it was the only thing to be done, unless it were to return to the camps north of the Rapidan. Every intelligent enlisted man in the Army of the Potomac knew that we could not wrest the Confederate intrenchments at Spottsylvania from Lee's veteran infantry.

Returning to the battery, I found many of the cannoneers studying war maps, with which we light-artillery men had abundantly supplied ourselves, and earnestly endeavoring to fathom Grant's plans. I had indulged in this military pastime with the infantry soldiers, and, when my comrades asked me to join them, I declined to waste further time in the sport, and spread my blankets under a tree on the vermin-infested ground, and was asleep instantly, to be awakened just as I was winning a great battle, by the drivers hitching in their horses. I packed up, asked a sergeant what time it was, and was told that it was about midnight. There were no bugle calls that night   Indeed, I heard no music, not even the tap of a drum.   Silently the battery rolled off of our camp ground.   We could hear the solid tread, tread, tread of un-seen infantry as they marched by.   All around us the air hummed and vibrated with life. Murmurs as of reeds whisperingly greeting the flowing sea filled the air.   We came to a broad road which showed white in the night, and along which the Second Corps were streaming at a swinging gait, with their arms at will.   We turned into the road and marched alongside of these men.   How they growled!   How they swore!   We, too, growled and marched, and growled and swore, and grumbled and enjoyed life right savagely.   About two o'clock in the morning we heard a noise in the forest to our right, and then a couple of rifle shots rang out sharply.   Instantly the column halted.   The infantry faced to the right, and crowded close to the cannon.   A score of men sprang over the guns, and dashed through the forest in the direction of the sound we had heard.   The rifles of the soldiers crowding us were raised to their shoulders.

"Lie down! lie down!" they whispered to us.

We unlimbered the guns, but had not sufficient space to swing them into battery, so closely did the infantry press around us.

"Lie down! Get out of our line of fire! Lie down!" whispered a soldier, whose eyes blazed with excitement, to me and to my comrades.

We crouched low around the gun-trails, and waited. After the column halted I did not hear an officer give a command. The enlisted men knew what to do, and did it instantly and without orders. It was an impressive sight that I saw above me: two lines of veteran infantry, with rifles almost aimed, with set faces and blazing eyes, gazing intently into the darkness of a dense forest in search of an unseen enemy whom we thought was lurking there. So profound was the silence that I could hear my heart beat. Soon we heard the voices of the skirmishers, who had rushed into the woods, calling lowly, but distinctly, as they returned:

"There is nothing there. Don't fire! don't fire! We are coming back." They rejoined the battle-line, which faced into column, and, limbering up, we resumed the march. But I did not understand the two rifle shots, and I did not like the way in which the battery got jammed on the road.

The night wore away. Morning came, and we cooked breakfast at fires made of fence rails. We were in the best agricultural region that I had seen in Virginia. Many negro slaves were working in the fields. Some of the slaves did not quit their work to look at us. I saw none drop their tools and hail us with vociferous shouts as liberators and eagerly join us, as I had been led to believe they would.

Many of the farm-houses we passed were mansions built of brick, and around which piazzas ran. On these women and children, and old, white-haired men stood in silent groups, and looked intently at us. I saw no young men, no white men fit for war, around any of these farm-houses. There were many barns and sheds and groups of negro quarters. We, the ever-hungry, predatory enlisted men, quickly discovered that we were marching through a corn- and tobacco and stock-raising country, and we raided tobacco barns in a quiet manner, and killed some sheep and many chickens, and much food was stolen from the farm-houses. I paid a pale-faced woman, whose little children clung to her skirts as she stood in her kitchen door appealing to the Union soldiers not to strip her of stores as she had children to feed, $2 in greenbacks for a piece of sweet bacon, which I had found in a barn, where an aged negro stood, solemnly assuring the predatory soldiers that there was not a bite of food on the place. This at a large brick house a mile or two outside of Bowling Green.

Before noon we came to the village of Bowling Green, where many pretty girls stood at cottage windows or doors, and even as close to the despised Yankees as the garden gates, and looked scornfully at us as we marched through the pretty town to kill their fathers and brothers. There was one very attractive girl, black-eyed and curly-haired, and clad in a scanty calico gown, who stood by a well in a house yard. She looked so neat, so fresh, so ladylike and pretty, that I ran through the open gate and asked her if I might fill my canteen with water from the well. And she, the haughty Virginia maiden, refused to notice me. She calmly looked through me and over me, and never by the slightest sign acknowledged my presence ; but I filled my canteen, and drank her health. I liked her spirit.

It was a weary march, but a march during which there was no straggling. We could look back from hill tops and see the long steel-tipped column stretching for miles behind us. There was some anxiety among the enlisted men, but not much, as we were confident that we would not be called upon to fight more than half of Lee's army, if we had to fight at all, and we believed that the Second Corps, which we judged to number 30,000 men, could whip an equal number of Confederates in the open. At least we could try it, and a fight of that character would have been an agreeable change from assaulting earthworks. At noon we halted for dinner, and spent an hour or two in cooking and eating, and in lying on the ground talking and smoking the good tobacco we had stolen, and in sleeping.

Again we marched. By the middle of the afternoon one of my comrades called my attention to a dust column which rose away off to our right behind the crest of a ridge, and which moved parallel with us. The news spread up and down the column that we had been outmarched, and that wherever we stopped there we would find Longstreet's corps. How did we know that Longstreet's soldiers were to oppose us? I cannot tell. But I record the fact that we did know it, as an instance of the accuracy of the information the enlisted men of the

Army of the Potomac possessed. That afternoon I dropped behind the battery to talk to
some country boys who were serving in an infantry regiment—boys who were raised in
Columbia County, New York, and who lived on
farms that surrounded my family's homestead.
To them I expressed my anxiety at being so
far in advance of the main army. I was promptly reassured and encouraged by a young line
sergeant, who said :

" That dust you see over yonder is kicked up
by Longstreet's men. They were on the Confederate right at Spottsylvania. As soon as
the Confederates missed the Second Corps
from the battle-line, they knew that we had
been dispatched on a flanking movement, and
Lee started Longstreet toward Richmond to
intercept us. Now we have been fighting
Longstreet's corps for two weeks and better,
and we all know that he has not more than
fifteen thousand soldiers. The Confederates
are not sufficiently numerous to fight us in the
open. Longstreet will not attack the Second
Corps unless he is heavily reinforced. There
lies our only danger. See here, Frank," he
said, as he laid his hand on my shoulder to call
my attention away from the dust column. " See

here. Listen to a little common-sense. Lee
knows that the Second Corps has been detached
from our main army. He knows that Grant
has not more than sixty-five thousand men re-
maining with him. " Now, my boy," he solemnly
said, "if Lee had a sufficient number of men in
his entire army to enable him to whip Grant's
sixty-five thousand, he would have jumped on
him savagely the very instant he discovered
that the Second Corps had been detached. The
fact that he has not sufficient men to whip
sixty-five-thousand Union soldiers is plainly indicated by that dust column. If Lee had fifty
thousand men he would probably risk a battle
with Grant's weakened army. He has not got
them. The only danger we are in, is that Lee
may be marching with his entire army to jump
on the Second Corps. If that is his plan, and
I think it is not, he had better put it into execution speedily, because in less than an hour
after we halt this evening we will be intrenched,
and once behind earthworks the Second Corps
can whip the entire Confederate army." The
line sergeant clearly expressed the thoughts
and feelings of all the intelligent volunteers. I
have quoted him to illustrate the accuracy of
military reasoning that enabled the enlisted

men of American blood to correctly judge of
the state of the campaign. How did the men
acquire their information? From prisoners
whom they captured, from fellow-soldiers serving in the cavalry, from negroes, and above all
from the "news-gatherers," the soldiers who
walked the battle-lines in the night.

Morally strengthened and braced up by the
sergeant's talk, I ran ahead and rejoined my
gun. Toward evening I saw troops defiling to
the left of the road ahead of us, and as soon as
they halted dirt began to fly and intrenchments
to rise out of the ground. My battery was directed to camp on a slight elevation, which a
staff officer indicated with a gleaming sabre.
We swung into battery. To our front and
right, distant about a thousand yards, was a
large white store, and near it stood a couple of
smaller buildings. The men of Battery K,
Fourth United States Artillery, which stood in
battery to our left, manned a gun, and almost
instantly a shell screamed through the air and
burst close to a group of Confederate scouts,
who sat on their horses in front of the white
store watching us. They disappeared, and I
saw no other Confederate soldiers at Milford
Station. Our line of defence was quickly

chosen, and at once the men began to fortify
it. Here they pushed the line out, there they
drew it back, taking advantage of the ground
and fortifying it as their experience had taught
them was best. In an hour a line of earthworks was thrown up which the Second Corps
could have held for days against all the Confederates whom Lee could have massed to the assault. To our left, distant about eight hundred
yards, and in a point of heavy oak timber, lay
an Irish brigade—tough, jovial fellows, and
stanch fighters. They built the crack intrenchment of the line.

The hard marching of the flank movement
was over. That night we slept, and the next
day we slept again and rested. North Anna
was ahead of us. The Wilderness and Spottsylvania, where so many of our comrades lay
dead on the ground, were of the past.

VII.

STUDYING CONFEDERATE EARTHWORKS AT NORTH ANNA.

MAY 23, 1864. The Army of the Potomac approached the North Anna River. In front of the Second Corps (Hancock's) was the Chesterfield wagon bridge, and a mile below a railroad bridge spanned the river. The wagon bridge was protected by a heavy but small earthwork on one side of the river. The rear of this work was open. It was full of men, but there were no guns in it. In front of it we could plainly see the Confederate pickets lying in their rifle-pits. The railroad bridge was protected by a heavy two-gun fortification standing on the other side of the river. A mile beyond the river the main line of Confederates lay in their trenches. While our troops were deploying, the battery I belonged to was ordered to take position on the crest of a ridge that overlooked the railroad bridge earthwork,

and to begin firing at once. The officer who
brought our captain this order dwelt strongly
on the necessity of haste in getting into action,
as the infantry, so he said, were to assault both
earthworks. I smiled at the absurd statement
that tired, exhausted infantry were to assault an
earthwork that lay on the other side of a deep
stream; but the pace at which the battery
moved caused the smile to fade from my face as
I ran at the side of my gun. We swung into
action on the crest of the ridge. The sponge
staffs were unchained, and the gunners quickly
sprang too and fro, in and out, from the guns,
and we opened the battle as far as the Second
Corps was concerned. There was a loud noise
behind us. I looked back as I sprang clear of
the muzzle of the gun I was serving and saw
other batteries galloping toward us. Bugles
were blown, officers shouted, and the guns went
into battery alongside of us, until about thirty
pieces surmounted the crest. Then a brigade
of infantry came marching up to support us.
There were not a sufficient number of Confederates on our side of the river, outside of the
Chesterfield works, to have captured a beehive,
let alone thirty pieces of artillery. We fired
rapidly and accurately at the sand-bank behind

which the Confederate artillerists lurked, and with the usual effect, of doing nothing. I saw shells burst all over the work and tiny clouds of dust rise from it, as though it were a big puff ball which we occasionally and gently squeezed. The rebel guns replied slowly. Thirty guns against two old howitzers! It was rather a one-sided fight, and the inequality was calculated to make the service of the howitzers rather slow, but still they were served. We could see the Confederate gunners rise out of the ground, could see them load and then sink out of sight, could see the gunner bend over the piece and then raise his hand to No. 4 ; instantly a cloud of smoke would shoot out of the gun, and from it a black ball would rise and come screeching toward us. We were, as I said, firing rapidly, and shell were bursting over the Confederate earthwork at the rate of about three in two seconds. We had got the range to an inch. The plain beyond the work was furrowed and torn with shell. The works must have quivered with the steady and heavy shocks. I can imagine no hotter place than that little fort was. I tired of my work, and asked a spare man to take the sponge while I rested. He cheerfully did so, and I sat on the

ground to one side of the battery, and filled a
pipe with plug tobacco, and smoked and
watched the Confederate earthwork through my
field-glass. I had about lost interest in the one-
sided affair, when I saw an officer on a milk-
white horse ride forth from the woods in the
rear of the Confederate work. Confident that
he would be torn to bits by shells, I dropped
my pipe, and glued my glass on him and
waited for the tragedy. He trotted briskly
over the plain where shell were thickly bursting,
and into the fort. I saw him hand a paper to
the officer in command of the work. He sat
calmly on his horse, and talked and gesticulated
as quietly as though he were on dress parade.
My heart went out to that man. I hoped he
would not be killed. I wished I had the aiming
of the guns. He lifted his hand in salute to
the visor of his cap. He turned his white
horse and rode slowly across the open ground,
where shot and shell were thickly coursing.
Dust rose above him. Tiny clouds of smoke
almost hid him from view. Shot struck the
ground and skipped past him, but he did not
urge his horse out of a walk. He rode as
though lost in meditation and deaf to the uproar that raged around him. He rode into the

woods, disappeared in the timber, and was safe. With a "Thank God that that brave man was not killed," I rejoined my gun and resumed work at the fruitless task of trying to batter down a sand-bank.

Below us to our right, infantry had taken position in a sheltered ravine. There were two thousand men lying down there. There were a few men along the crest of the ravine on the side next to the Chesterfield bridge head, and they continually made motions to their comrades who were lying in the bottom. Farther to the right were two sections of artillery in action. They were firing rapidly at the bridge head, which did not answer. We pounded away at our fort for a couple of hours longer, then, about six o'clock, I heard the familiar charging cheer. Looking to the right I saw a heavy line of blue-coated infantry move swiftly forth from a forest, and rapidly run at the fort in a fairly good line. The Confederate pickets fired and then ran to their fortification, which instantly began to smoke in jets and puffs and curls as an immense pudding, and men in the blue-coated line fell headlong, or backward, or sank into little heaps. The charging infantry, Price's and Eagan's brigades of the Second Corps, were accompanied by an officer on horseback, who, in the most gallant manner rode his horse up and down the charging line and bravely encouraged his men, and excited the admiration of the artillerymen who saw him. Then the brigade in the ravine stood up and remained quiet. They were to make the second assault in case the first failed I suppose; but the first did not fail. They swept on and ran over the earthwork, out of which the Confederate infantry ran, and streamed across the bridge. Our colors were on the work. We cheered, and our supports cheered. And then a fierce charging yell floated to us from the right, and smoke began to curl above the portion of the line held by the Fifth Corps. Then there was real fighting going on, not driving two hundred or four hundred men out of an earthwork by launching several thousand picked troops against them. We could see a part of the fight the Fifth Corps was engaged in, and could see that they had a hard struggle. It was as gallant a fight as ever I saw; but the Fifth Corps got decidedly the worst of it, and came mighty near being driven into the river. We were very anxious about this fighting, as we always were about heavy fighting that we did not share in. The

unseen danger is the alarming one to the enlisted men. Before midnight two privates of
the Twentieth Maine Infantry, then serving
with Griffin's division of the Fifth Corps, came
into the battery to gather news. They told us
that the Fifth Corps had been surprised ; that
they had been ordered at five o'clock to biv-
ouac on the line they held, and that at that
hour General Warren was soundly sleeping in a
house north of the river and near the Jericho
ford. They said that the adjutant of their
regiment had twice crossed the river to carry
word to Warren from General Griffin that the
Confederates were massing for the attack, and
that the first time he was unable to see Warren,
being refused admittance to his room, and that
on the second visit he was so vehement in his
demands that he was admitted to the presence
of the general, who snubbed him, and told him
that the rebels would not attack; and after
ordering the troops to camp on the line, he
turned over and slept. The adjutant returned
to Griffin and reported, and had hardly done so
when the Confederate assault was delivered.
These intelligent Yankee infantrymen assured
us that this story of the negligence of Warren
was true, and that Griffin's division had saved

the Fifth Corps from rout when the battle
opened, and that later, when Hill massed
against Cutler's division and broke it with a
savage blow, Colonel McCoy, with the Eighty-
third Pennsylvania, caught the Confederate
charging column in flank and whipped them
and captured over one thousand prisoners.
"And haggard, hungry-looking men they are,
too," said one of our Yankee visitors. "Boys,"
he added impressively, "we are not living on
the fat of the land; but I looked into the haversacks of some of Hill's men as they passed to
the rear, and none of them had more than a
couple of handfuls of corn-meal in their canvas
sacks. How they fight on corn-meal straight
is more than I can understand," he added re-
flectively. Our visitors arose, cast their eyes
around in search of a full haversack, and, seeing
that we regarded their inquisitive glances with
hostile eyes, they laughed and walked off, first
inviting us to visit them when they got into
permanent camp and eat doughnuts.

Next morning we crossed the river. We
passed the fort which we had bombarded the
previous day. Two men with shovels could
have repaired the damage it had suffered in two
hours, and we had buried tons of good iron in

it. As soon as we drew away from the river bank and reached a point where we could plainly see the Confederate lines, we saw that Lee's soldiers were skilfully intrenched and that the Army of the Potomac could not dislodge them. That fact was instantly comprehended by the enlisted men who inspected the works at close range. We threw up parallel intrenchments and impatiently waited for our generals to discover that the position could not be forced. The Confederate line was much shorter than ours, and was shaped like a wide-opened ox-bow. They could have supplied troops to any point attacked. Our men shrank from assaulting these works. The pickets had been close to them, and they one and all asserted that the position was impregnable when held by the Army of Northern Virginia.

One day, as we lay in our earthworks under a sharpshooters' fire, I saw a civilian clad in a long linen duster ride toward our battery. I thought he had a queer idea of a pleasure trip. To my great amazement he rode into the battery and asked if I were present. I was, and promptly said so. "Well, if you are the man, and I guess you are, here is a package of tobacco your father has sent to you," he said, handing me a couple of pounds of plug tobacco. This, under a brisk picket and sharpshooters' fire. He dismounted from his horse and stood by his side, and talked to me for a moment or two, and I heartily wished he would go away. He told me that he was a *New York Tribune* corspondent. He smiled, pointed to a couple of dead men, and said, as he raised his eyebrows inquiringly : " Rather warm here, eh ? Sharpshooters got the range, but," looking toward the woods where those murderous men lurked, " it is a long shot." Then he bade me good-by, and coolly mounted and deliberately rode off.

One day some men of the Fortieth New York Infantry came to my battery to gamble. I took a hand in a game of seven-up for a dollar a corner and five on the rubber. We spread a blanket on the ground behind the earthworks and squatted around it. My partner, a Fortieth New York soldier, was a heavy-jawed light-haired, blue-eyed lad of nineteen, an Albany boy, who played well, and fought well too. He was a wit, and when in the humor would make a whole regiment of sick men laugh. We were a few dollars winners, and he was graphically and humorously describing the brigade of regulars running against a swamp in the Wilderness, and the mythical conversation between the gray-haired commander and the second lieutenant, just out of West Point, as the old soldier asked if there was any thing in the new books about getting a brigade across a swamp, was delicious. As we laughed the handsome lad fell face down into the blanket and began to vomit blood. We grabbed him, turned him over, tore up his shirt, and saw where a ball had entered his side, cutting a gash instead of a hole. The wounded soldier did not speak. The blood rushed out of his mouth, his eyes glazed, his jaw dropped — he was dead. A chance ball had struck the tire of one of the wheels of the No. 1 gun and glanced forward and killed this delightful comrade. His death ended the game. We put his body alongside of a couple of other dead men and buried the three that night.

The picket-firing and sharpshooting at North Anna was exceedingly severe and murderous. We were greatly annoyed by it, and as a campaign cannot be decided by killing a few hundred enlisted men—killing them most unfairly and when they were of necessity exposed,—it did seem as though the sharpshooting pests should have been suppressed. Our sharpshooters were as bad as the Confederates, and neither of them were of any account as far as decisive results were obtained. They could sneak around trees or lurk behind stumps, or cower in wells or in cellars, and from the safety of their lairs murder a few men. Put the sharpshooters in battle-line and they were no better, no more effective, than the infantry of the line, and they were not half as decent. There was an unwritten code of honor among the infantry that forbade the shooting of men while attending to the imperative calls of nature, and these sharpshooting brutes were constantly violating that rule. I hated sharpshooters, both Confederate and Union, in those days, and I was always glad to see them killed.

Before we left North Anna I discovered that our infantry were tired of charging earthworks. The ordinary enlisted men assert that one good man behind an earthwork was equal to three good men outside of it, and that they did not propose to charge many more intrenched lines. Here I first heard savage protests against a continuance of the generalship which consisted in launching good troops against intrenched works which the generals had not inspected. Battle-tried privates came into the battery and sneeringly inquired if the corps and army commanders had been to see our line. Of course we replied " No." " Well," said one sergeant of the Pennsylvania reserve, " I have fought in this army for three years, and in no other campaign have I seen so many general officers shirk as they have in this one. I saw the Confederate lines at close range last night," he added, " and they cannot be assaulted with any prospect of success. If Grant, or Meade, or Hancock, or Warren, or Wright, or Burnside would inspect those works at close range, they would see the folly of staying here, where we are losing two hundred or three hundred men every day by sharpshooters. We ought to get out of here and try it farther down." He but expressed what we all thought. At North Anna the rank and file of the Potomac army, the men who did the fighting, and who had been under fire for three weeks, began to grow discouraged.

We lay for three days in the trenches at North Anna. Three days of woe and sorrow and hardship. Three days, during which there had been some exceedingly severe fighting, and which had cost us hundreds of men and line officers. How we longed to get away from

North Anna, where we had not the slightest chance of success, and how we feared that Grant would keep sending us to the slaughter! Joyfully we received the order to march on the night of May 26th. Eagerly the tired troops fell into line behind their foul intrenchments. With pleasure we recrossed the North Anna and resumed the flank movement to the south. That night, after crossing the river, we rested, and had a good night's sleep, undisturbed by picket-firing. We awoke the next morning to find the rest of the army gone, and we started after them, being for the first and last time during the campaign in the rear. Before us, in the distance, rose the swells of Cold Harbor, and we marched steadily and joyfully to our doom.

VIII.

THE BATTLE OF COLD HARBOR.

ON the morning of May 28, 1864, the Second Corps crossed the Pamunkey River. Close by the bridge on which we crossed, and to the right of it, under a tree, stood Generals Grant, Meade, and Hancock, and a little back of them was a group of staff officers. Grant looked tired. He was sallow. He held a dead cigar firmly between his teeth. His face was as expressionless as a pine board. He gazed steadily at the enlisted men as they marched by, as though trying to read their thoughts, and they gazed intently at him. He had the power to send us to our deaths, and we were curious to see him. But the men did not evince the slightest enthusiasm. None cheered him, none saluted him. Grant stood silently looking at his troops and listening to Hancock, who was talking and gesticulating earnestly. Meade stood by Grant's side and thoughtfully stroked his own face. I stepped from the column and filled my canteens in the Pamunkey River, and looked my fill at the generals and their staffs, and then ran by the marching troops through a gantlet of chaff, as " Go it, artillery," " The artillery is advancing," " Hurry to your gun, my son, or the battle will be lost," and similar sarcastically good-natured remarks, which were calculated to stimulate my. speed.

During the afternoon we heard considerable firing in front of us, and toward evening we marched over ground where dead cavalrymen were plentifully sprinkled. The blue and the gray lay side by side, and their arms by them. With the Confederates lay muzzle-loading carbines, the ramrods of which worked upward on a swivel hinge fastened near the muzzle of the weapon. It was an awkward arm and far inferior to the Spencer carbine with which our cavalry was armed. There were ancient and ferocious-looking horse-pistols, such as used to grace the Bowery stage, lying by the dead Confederates. The poverty of the South was plainly shown by the clothing and equipment of her dead. These dead men were hardly stiff when we saw them. All of their pockets had been turned inside out. That night, while searching for fresh, clean water, I found several dead cavalrymen in the woods, where they had probably crawled after being wounded. I struck a match so as to see one of these men plainly, and was greatly shocked to see large black beetles eating the corpse. I looked at no more dead men that night.

The next day the sound of battle arose again. At distant points it would break out furiously and then die down. In our immediate front heavy skirmishing was going on, and wounded men began to drift to the rear in search of hospitals. They said that there was a stream of water, swamps, and a line of earthworks, behind which lay the Confederate infantry, in our front, and that we could not get to the works. At no time did the fire rise to a battle's volume ; it was simply heavy and continuous skirmishing, in which our men fought at great disadvantage, and were severely handled. Finding that these works were too strong to be taken by assault, Grant moved the army to the left. On June 1st we heard heavy fighting to our left, and that night we learned that a portion of the Sixth Corps, aided by ten thousand of Butler's men from Bermuda Hundreds, had forced the Chickahominy River at a loss of three thousand men, and that they held the ground they had taken. The news-gatherers said that the Confederates were strongly intrenched, and evidently had no intention of fighting in the open. We knew that a bloody battle was close at hand, and instead of being elated the enlisted men were depressed in spirits. That night the old soldiers told the story of the campaign under McClellan in 1862. They had fought over some of the ground we were then camped on. Some of the men were sad, some indifferent; some so tired of the strain on their nerves that they wished they were dead and their troubles over. The infantry knew that they were to be called upon to assault perfect earthworks, and though they had resolved to do their best, there was no eagerness for the fray, and the impression among the intelligent soldiers was that the task cut out for them was more than men could accomplish.

On June 2d the Second Corps moved from the right to the left. We saw many wounded men that day. We crossed a swamp or marched around a swamp, and the battery I belonged to parked in a ravine. There were some old houses on our line of march, but not a chicken or a sheep or a cow to be seen. The land was wretchedly poor. The night of June 2d was spent in getting into battle-line.   There was considerable confusion as the infantry marched in the darkness.   In our front we could see tongues of flames dart forth from Confederate rifles as their pickets fired in the direction of the noise they heard, and their bullets sang high above our heads.   My battery went into position just back of a crest of a hill.   Behind us was an alder swamp, where good drinking water gushed forth from many springs.   Before we slept we talked with some of the Seventh New York Heavy Artillery, and found that they were sad of heart.   They knew that they were to go into the fight early in the morning, and they dreaded the work. The whole army seemed to be greatly depressed the night before the battle of Cold Harbor.

Before daybreak of June 3d the light-artillery men were aroused.   We ate our scanty breakfast and took our positions around the guns. All of us were loath to go into action.   In front of us we could hear the murmurs of infantry, but it was not sufficiently light to see them.   We stood leaning against the cool guns, or resting easily on the ponderous wheels, and gazed intently into the darkness in the direction of the Confederate earthworks. How slowly dawn came! Indistinctly we saw moving figures. Some on foot rearward bound, cowards hunting for safety; others on horseback riding to and fro near where we supposed the battle-lines to be; then orderlies and servants came in from out the darkness leading horses, and we knew that the regimental and brigade commanders were going into action on foot. The darkness faded slowly, one by one the stars went out, and then the Confederate pickets opened fire briskly; then we could see the Confederate earthworks, about six hundred yards ahead of us—could just see them and no more. They were apparently deserted, not a man was to be seen behind them; but it was still faint gray light. One of our gunners looked over his piece and said that he could see the sights, but that they blurred. We filled our sponge buckets with water and waited, the Confederate pickets firing briskly at us the while, but doing no damage. Suddenly the Confederate works were manned. We could see a line of slouch hats above the parapet. Smoke in great puffs burst forth from their line, and shell began to howl by us. Their gunners were getting the range. We sprung in and out from the three-inch guns and replied angrily. To our left, to our right, other batteries opened; and along the Confederate line cannon sent forth their balls searching for the range. Then their guns were silent. It was daylight. We, the light-artillery men, were heated with battle. The strain on our nerves was over. In our front were two lines of blue-coated infantry. One well in advance of the other, and both lying down. We were firing over them. The Confederate pickets sprang out of their rifle pits and ran back to their main line of works. Then they turned and warmed the battery with long-range rifle practice, knocking a man over here, killing another there, breaking the leg of a horse yonder, and generally behaving in an exasperating manner. The Confederate infantry was always much more effective than their artillery, and the battery that got under the fire of their cool infantry always suffered severely. The air began to grow hazy with powder smoke. We saw that the line of slouch-hatted heads had disappeared from the Confederate earthworks, leaving heads exposed only at long intervals. Out of the powder smoke came an officer from the battle-lines of infantry. He told us to stop firing, as the soldiers were about to charge. He disappeared to carry the message to other batteries. Our cannon became silent. The smoke drifted off of the field. I noticed that the sun was not yet up. Suddenly the foremost line of our troops, which were lying on the ground in front of us, sprang to their feet and dashed at the Confederate earthworks at a run. Instantly those works were manned. Cannon belched forth a torrent of canister, the works glowed brightly with musketry, a storm of lead and iron struck the blue line, cutting gaps in it. Still they pushed on, and on, and on. But, how many of them fell! They drew near the earthworks, firing as they went, and then, with a cheer, the first line of the Red Division of the Second Corps (Barlow's) swept over it. And there in our front lay, sat, and stood the second line, the supports; why did not they go forward and make good the victory? They did not. Intensely excited, I watched the portion of the Confederate line which our men had captured. I was faintly conscious of terrific firing to our right and of heavy and continuous cheering on that portion of our line which was held by the Fifth and Sixth Corps. For once the several corps had delivered a simultaneous assault, and I knew that it was to be

now or never. The powder smoke curled
lowly in thin clouds above the captured works.
Then the firing became more and more thunderous. The tops of many battle-flags could
be seen indistinctly, and then there was a heavy
and fierce yell, and the thrilling battle-cry of the
Confederate infantry floated to us. "Can our
men withstand the charge?" I asked myself.
Quickly I was answered. They came into sight
clambering over the parapet of the captured
works. All organization was lost. They fled
wildly for the protection of their second line
and the Union guns, and they were shot by
scores as they ran. The Confederate infantry
appeared behind their works and nimbly climbed
over, as though intent on following up their
success, and their fire was as the fury of hell.
We manned the guns and drove them to cover
by bursting shell. How they yelled! How
they swung their hats! And how quickly their
pickets ran forward to their rifle pits and sank
out of sight! The swift, brave assault had
been bravely met and most bloodily repulsed.
Twenty minutes had not passed since the infantry had sprung to their feet, and ten-thou-
sand of our men lay dead or wounded on the
ground. The men of the Seventh New York

Heavy Artillery came back without their colonel. The regiment lost heavily in enlisted men and line officers. Men from many commands sought shelter behind the crest of the hill we were behind. They seemed to be dazed and utterly discouraged. They told of the strength of the Confederate earthworks, and asserted that behind the line we could see was another and stronger line, and all the enlisted men insisted that they could not have taken the second line even if their supports had followed them. These battle-dazed visitors drifted off after a while and found their regiments, but some of them drifted to the rear and to coffee pots. We drew the guns back behind the crest of the hill, and lay down in the sand and waited. I noticed that the sun was now about a half an hour high. Soldiers came to the front from the rear, hunting for their regiments, which had been practically annihilated as offensive engines of war. Occasionally a man fell dead, struck by a stray ball from the picket line. By noon the stragglers were mostly gathered up and had rejoined their regiments, and columns of troops began to move to and fro in our rear in the little valley formed by the alder swamp. A column of infantry marching by fours passed to our right.   I watched them, listlessly wondering if they were going to get something to eat, as I was hungry.   I saw a puff of smoke between the marchers and myself, heard the report of a bursting shell, and twelve men of that column were knocked to the earth.   Their officers shouted, " Close up ! close up ! "   The uninjured men hurriedly closed the gap and marched on.   The dead and wounded men lay on the ground, with their rifles scattered among them.

Soon some soldiers came out of the woods and carried the wounded men off, but left the dead where they fell.   We buried them that night. Then, as the day wore away, and the troops were well in hand again, I saw staff officers ride along the lines, and then I saw the regimental commanders getting their men into line.   About four o'clock in the afternoon I heard the charging commands given.   With many an oath at the military stupidity which would again send good troops to useless slaughter, I sprang to my feet and watched the doomed infantry.   Men, whom I knew well, stood rifle in hand not more than thirty feet from me, and I am happy to state that they continued to so stand.   Not a man stirred from his place.   The army to a man refused to obey the order, presumably from General Grant, to renew the assault. I heard the order given, and I saw it disobeyed. Many of the enlisted men had been up to and over the Confederate works. They had seen their strength, and they knew that they could not be taken by direct assault, and they refused to make a second attempt. That night we began to intrench.

By daylight we had our earthwork finished and were safe. The Seventh New York Heavy Artillery, armed as infantry, were intrenched about eighty yards in front of us. We were on the crest of a ridge ; they were below us. Behind us, for supports, were two Delaware regiments, their combined strength being about one hundred and twenty men. Back of us was the alder swamp, where springs of cool water gushed forth. The men in front of us had to go to these springs for water. They would draw lots to see who should run across the dangerous, bullet-swept ground that intervened between our earthworks and theirs. This settled, the victim would hang fifteen or twenty canteens around him ; then, crouching low in the rifle-pits, he would give a great jump, and when he struck the ground he was running at the top of his speed for our earthwork. Every Confederate sharpshooter within range fired at him. Some of these thirsty men were shot dead; but generally they ran into the earthwork with a laugh. After filling their canteens, they would sit by our guns and smoke and talk, nerving themselves for the dangerous return. Adjusting their burden of canteens, they would go around the end of our works on a run and rush back over the bullet-swept course, and again every Confederate sharpshooter who saw them would fire at them. Sometimes these water-carriers would come to us in pairs. One day two Albany men leaped into our battery. After filling their canteens, they sat with us and talked of the beautiful city on the Hudson, and finally started together for their rifle-pits. I watched through an embrasure, and saw one fall. Instantly he began to dig a little hollow with his hands in the sandy soil, and instantly the Confederate sharpshooters went to work at him. The dust flew up on one side of him, and then on the other. The wounded soldier kept scraping his little protective trench in the sand. We called to him. He answered that his leg was broken below the knee by a rifle ball. From the rifle-pits we heard his comrades call to him to take off his burden of canteens, to tie their strings together, and to set them to one side. He did so, and then the thirsty men in the pits drew lots to see who should risk his life for the water. I got keenly interested in this dicing with death, and watched intently. A soldier sprang out of the rifle-pits. Running obliquely, he stooped as he passed the canteens, grasped the strings, turned, and in a flash was safe. Looking through the embrasure, I saw the dust rise in many little puffs around the wounded man, who was still digging his little trench, and, with quickening breath, felt that his minutes were numbered. I noted a conspicuous man, who was marked with a goitre, in the rifle-pits, and recognized him as the comrade of the stricken soldier. He called to his disabled friend, saying that he was coming for him, and that he must rise when he came near and cling to him when he stopped. The hero left the rifle-pits on the run; the wounded man rose up and stood on one foot; the runner clasped him in his arms; the arms of the wounded man twined around his neck, and he was carried into our battery at full speed, and was hurried to the rear and to a hospital. To the honor of the Confederate sharpshooters, be it said, that when they understood what was being done they ceased to shoot.

One day during this protracted Cold Harbor fight, a battery of Cohorn mortars was placed in position in the ravine behind us. The captain of this battery was a tall, handsome, sweet-voiced man. He spent a large portion of his time in our earthworks, watching the fire of his mortars. He would jump on a gun and look over the works, or he would look out through the embrasures. Boy-like, I talked to him. I would have talked to a field-marshal if I had met one. He told me many things relative to mortar practice, and I, in turn, showed him how to get a fair look at the Confederate lines without exposing himself to the fire of the sharp-shooters, most of whom we had "marked down." He playfully accused me of being afraid, and insisted that at six hundred yards a sharpshooter could not hit a man. But I had seen too many men killed in our battery to believe that. So he continued to jump on guns and to poke his head into embrasures. One day I went to the spring after water. While walking back I met four men carrying a body in a blanket. "Who is that?" I asked. "The captain of the mortars," was the reply.

Stopping, they uncovered his head for me. I saw where the ball had struck him in the eye, and saw the great hole in the back of his head where it had passed out.

The killed and wounded of the first day's fight lay unburied and uncared for between the lines. The stench of the dead men became unbearable, and finally a flag of truce was sent out. There was a cessation of hostilities to bury the dead and to succor the wounded. I went out to the ground in front of our picket line to talk to the Confederate soldiers, and to trade sugar and coffee for tobacco. Every corpse I saw was as black as coal. It was not possible to remove them. They were buried where they fell. Our wounded—I mean those who had fallen on the first day on the ground that lay between the picket lines—were all dead. I saw no live man lying on this ground. The wounded must have suffered horribly before death relieved them, lying there exposed to the blazing southern sun o' days, and being eaten alive by beetles o' nights.

One evening just before sunset I went to the spring to fill some canteens. Having filled them, I loaded my pipe and smoked in silent enjoyment. Looking up, I saw two Confeder-

ate infantry soldiers walking slowly down the
ravine. They were tall, round-shouldered men.
I clasped my knees and stared at them. They
walked toward me, then halted, and dropping
their musket-butts to the ground, they clasped
their hands over the muzzles of their rifles and
stared at me as I stared at them. I could not
understand what two fully armed Confederate
soldiers could be doing within our lines. After
gazing at one another in silence for an instant,
one of them smiled (I could almost hear the
dirt on his face crack, and was agreeably interested in the performance) and inquired kindly,
"Howdy?" So I said, still seated and sucking my pipe, "Howdy," as that seemed to be
the correct form of salutation in Virginia.
Then I asked indifferently what they were
doing within our lines. They told me that
they had been captured and that they were on
their way to our rear. That statement struck
me as decidedly funny. I did not believe it,
and my face expressed my disbelief. They
then said that they were lost, that they were
afraid to return to the front for fear of being
killed, that they were afraid to keep on travel-
ling for fear of running against the Union pickets on the flanks, and that they were out of

provisions and were hungry. That last statement appealed strongly to me. I imagined myself prowling between the front and the rear of
the Confederate army, with an empty haversack
dangling at my side, and nothing to hope for
but a Confederate prison, and my heart went
out to these men. I opened my haversack and
shared my hardtack with them, and then showed
them the road which led to our rear. They
sat down by the spring and ate the hard bread
and drank of the cool water, and talked drawlingly of the war, and finally slouched off
to the rear. At the time I thought them to
be deserters. After dark, to replenish the
waste of my charity, I visited the camp of
some 100-day men, and found a half-filled
haversack. It was surprising what careless
fellows those 100-day men were. They were
always losing something, haversacks generally,
and we light-artillery men were constantly
finding them.

During the fighting of the fourth day, which
was not severe, a head-quarters' orderly rode
into the battery and delivered an order to our
captain. He read it, and then calling me to
him, handed me the order to read. With military brevity it commanded him to send Private

Frank Wilkeson to army head-quarters at once to report to Adjutant-General Seth Williams. My heart sank. I had been stealing haversacks. I had been exceedingly impudent to some officers. I had been doing a lot of things which I should not have done, and now I was in for it. "Adjutant-General," I repeated thoughtfully to myself. "That sounds rather savage." The captain said: "Wash up and accompany the orderly. Get a horse from the chief of caissons and return promptly."

I ignored the first portion of the order, but secured the horse and rode off, pants in boots slouch-hatted, flannel-shirted, blouseless, a strap around my waist and supremely dirty. I was tortured with the belief that I was to be punished. A certain sheep, which I had met in a field near Bowling Green, weighed heavily on me. A large bunch of haversacks, which I had found o' nights, dangled before me. I ransacked my memory and dragged forth all my military misdeeds and breaches of discipline and laid them one after the other on my saddle-bow and thoughtfully turned them over and over and looked at them, regretfully at first, then desperately and recklessly. I knew that I ought to be court-martialed and that I deserved to be shot. I talked to the orderly, and asked what duties the adjutant-general performed (I had an idea that he shot insubordinate privates), and was immensely relieved to hear that he was the officer who issued orders—a very superior order of chief clerk, as it were. "Is he savage-tempered?" I asked. "Who, General Williams?" my guide exclaimed in questioning surprise. "Not he," he answered; "he is the kindest-hearted man in the army." I was slightly reassured.

I said: "See here, what do you suppose he wants of me? I do not know him and I do not want to know him. I have been disobeying orders, been stealing haversacks from infantry soldiers, and have been impudent to some incompetent officers. You do not suppose that I have been reported to head-quarters, do you?"

Loudly the orderly laughed and roundly he swore, and then he said: "Not at all. No one cares how many haversacks you have stolen, excepting the men who lost them; and as for being impudent to some of these officers, they deserve it. You need not be troubled. When a private is sent for and guided to head-quarters, he is not going to be hurt."

We rode into a village of tents, one of which was pointed out to me as General Williams'. Sentinels paced to and fro; nice, clean men they were too.   I dismounted, hitched my horse, and walked to Williams' tent.   I was halted, sent in my name, and was admitted. I strode in defiant, hat on head, expecting to be abused, and resolved to take a hand in the abuse business myself.   Boy that I was, I was really frightened half out of my senses.

I saw a handsome, kind-faced, middle-aged officer standing before me.   He smiled kindly, and inquired, as he extended his hand to me, "Have I the pleasure of addressing Lieutenant Frank Wilkeson?"   My hat came off instantly; my heart went out to Seth Williams, and I replied: "No, General; I am Private Frank Wilkeson."   He smiled again and looked curiously at me.   How I did wish I had washed my face and brushed the dirt off of my clothes. He bade me to be seated, and skilfully set me to talking.   He asked me many questions, and I answered as intelligently as I could.   Growing confidential, I told him that I had been dreadfully frightened by being summoned to head-quarters, and confessed the matters of the sheep and the haversacks, and my misconception of his duties. He tried to look severely grave, but laughed instead, and said pleasantly: "You are not to be shot. The crimes you have committed hardly deserve that punishment. I have called you to me to say that Secretary of War Stanton has ordered your discharge, and that you are to be appointed a second lieuten-ant·in the Fourth Regiment of United States Artillery. When you want your discharge, claim it from your captain. He has the order to discharge you. When you get it, come to me if you need money to travel on, and I will lend you sufficient to take you to Washington and to buy you some clothing. When you arrive there, report to the Secretary of War, and he will tell you what to do."

Kind Seth Williams! So gracious, and sweet, and sympathetic was he to me, a dirty private, that my eyes filled with tears, and I could not talk, could not thank him. I came within an ace of crying outright. I returned to my battery and resumed work on my gun. I thought that the Army of the Potomac might win the next battle, and end the war. If it did, I preferred to be a private in a volunteer battery which was serving at the front, rather than to be a lieutenant in the United States

Artillery, stationed at Camp Barry, near Washington.

On one of these six Cold Harbor days, when my battery was in action, I saw a party of horsemen riding toward us from the left. I smiled as the absurdity of men riding along a battle-line for pleasure filled my sense of the ridiculous; but as I looked I saw that the party consisted of a civilian under escort. The party passed close behind our guns, and in passing the civilian exposed a large placard, which was fastened to his back, and which bore the words, "Libeler of the Press." We all agreed that he had been guilty of some dreadful deed, and were pleased to see him ride the battle-line. He was howled at, and the wish to tear him limb from limb and strew him over the ground was fiercely expressed. This man escaped death from the shot and shells and bullets that filled the air. I afterward met him in Washington, and he told me that he was a newspaper war correspondent, and that his offence was in writing, as he thought, truthfully, to his journal, that General Meade advised General Grant to retreat to the north of the Rapidan after the battle of the Wilderness.

One night, of these six Cold Harbor nights,

I was on guard in the battery. I walked up and down behind the guns. Voices whispering outside of our work startled me. Then I heard men scrambling up the face of the earthwork. In the indistinct light I made out four. They were carrying something. They stood above me on the parapet, and in reply to my challenge poked fun at me. They said they loved me, and had brought me a present. They threw down to me a dead man, and with a light laugh went off. I called to them to come back—insisted that they should carry their corpse and bury it, but they stood off in the darkness and laughed at me, and insisted that they had made me a present of him. " You can have him ; the battery can have him," and disappeared, leaving the dead man with me.

I was young, and therefore soft ; and the lack of good food and loss of sleep told hard on me. Indeed, I got utterly used up. So one afternoon of this battle that lasted nearly a week, when but little was going on, I said to my sergeant : " I am exhausted, and want a night's sleep. I will dig a trench back here. If possible, let me sleep to-night, or I will be on the sick-list." He promised to let me sleep unless something urgent happened in the night.

I ate my supper, wrapped my blanket around me, and lay down in my trench. The guns roared about me, the bullets whistled over me; but, overcome with exhaustion, I fell into a deep sleep. I was awakened with a strong grip on my shoulders, was lifted up and violently shaken, and the earnest voice of the gunner told me to run to my gun. " They have got an enfilading fire on us," the sergeant cried to me. Dazed, half awake, stupid from the deep sleep and coming sickness, I sat on the brink of my trench and wondered where I was. I heard, " Ho, Frank! Yah! No. 1!" sharply screamed. I heard the shot crash into our horses. Still not awake, I started for my gun. I saw the blaze of the fuses of the shells as they whizzed by. I saw countless fireflies; and, in my exhausted, half-awake condition, I confounded the shells and fireflies together, and thought they were all shells. The shock to me, in my weak, nervous condition, when I saw, as I thought, the air actually stiff with shells, required all my pride to stand up under. It woke me up and left me with a fit of trembling that required ten minutes warm work at the guns to get rid of. The enfilading fire did not amount to much, and I soon returned to my trench and deep sleep.

One day four men carrying a pale infantry-man stopped for an instant in my battery. The wounded man suffered intensely from a wound through the foot. My sympathy was excited for the young fellow, and as we at the moment were doing nothing, I asked for half an hour's leave. Getting it, I accompanied him back into the woods to one of the Second Corps' field hospitals. Here, groaning loudly, he awaited his turn, which soon came. We lifted him on the rude table. A surgeon held chloroform to his nostrils, and under its influence he lay as if in death. The boot was removed, then the stocking, and I saw a great ragged hole on the sole of the foot where the ball came out. Then I heard the coatless surgeon who was making the examination cry out, "The cowardly whelp!" So I edged around and looked over the shoulders of an assistant surgeon, and saw that the small wound on the top of the foot, where the ball entered, was blackened with powder! I, too, muttered "The coward" and was really pleased to see the knife and saw put to work and the craven's leg taken off below the knee. He was carried into the shade of a tree, and left there to wake up. I watched the skilful surgeons probe and carve other patients.

The little pile of legs and arms grew steadily, while I waited for the object of my misplaced sympathy to recover his senses.   With a long breath he opened his eyes.   I was with him at once, and looked sharply at him.   I will never forget the look of horror that fastened on his face when he found his leg was off.   Utter hopelessness and fear that look expressed.   I entered into conversation with him ; and he, weakened and unnerved by the loss of the leg, and the chloroform, for once told the truth.   Lying on his back, he aimed at his great toe, meaning to shoot it off ; but being rudely joggled by a comrade at the critical instant, his rifle covered his foot just below the ankle, and an ounce ball went crashing through the bones and sinews. The wound, instead of being a furlough, was a discharge from the army, probably into eternity. Our guns at the front began to howl at the Confederates again, and I was forced to leave the hospital.   So I hastened back to my guns.   The utter contempt of the surgeons, their change from careful handling to almost brutality, when they discovered the wound was self-inflicted, was bracing to me.   I liked it, and rammed home the ammunition in gun No. 1 with vim.

Constantly losing men in our earthwork,

shot not in fair fight, but by sharpshooters, we all began to loathe the place. At last, one afternoon the captain ordered us to level the corn-hills between the battery and the road, so that we could withdraw the guns without making a noise. At once understanding that a flank movement was at hand, we joyfully gathered up shovels and spades, and went at the obstructions with a will. No. 3 of No. 1 gun, an Albany man, was at my side. I was bent over shovelling. I straightened myself up. He leaned over to sink his shovel, pitched forward in a heap, dead, and an artilleryman beyond him clasped his stomach and howled a death howl. No. 3 was shot from temple to temple. The ball passed through his head and hit the other man in the stomach, fatally wounding him. They were the last men our battery lost at Cold Harbor.

That evening the horses were brought up, and all the guns but mine, No. 1, were taken off. We sat and watched them disappear in the darkness. Soon heavy columns of infantry could be indistinctly seen marching by the alder swamp in our rear. Then all was quiet, excepting the firing of the pickets. We sat and waited for the expected advance of the Confederates; but they did not come. Towards midnight an officer rode into the earthwork and asked lowly who was in command. The sergeant stepped forward and received his orders. Turning to us he whispered, " Limber to the rear." Silently the horses swung around. The gun was limbered, and, with the caisson in the lead, we pulled out of the earthwork, slowly drove across the cornfield, struck into a dusty road in the forest, and marched for the James River and the bloody disasters that awaited us beyond that beautiful stream.

IX.

FIGHTING AROUND PETERSBURG.

ON the night of June 14, 1864, the battery to which I belonged went into park close to the James River, but not within sight of it. I well remember the camping ground, because I endeavored to get water out of a large spring which gushed from beneath a wide-spreading tree, which stood to the rear and right of a plantation house, where either a division or corps head-quarters had been established. The spring flowed freely. It had been boxed, and there was plenty of water for thousands of men in the box. The water in the sluggish runs had been roiled by artillery horses drinking, and been additionally befouled by hundreds of vermin-infested men bathing in it. The water in the spring was clear and cool, and I, with a dozen of my comrades, wanted some of it, but we did not get it. An alert sentinel stood over this water. He had orders to keep the waters of the spring sacred, to keep them unpolluted by the touch of enlisted men's canteens or coffee pots. At the time I protested savagely against the official selfishness which denied the use of the only clean water in the region to the men who did the fighting. The sentinel was ashamed to keep us from the water, but, as he said, he had to obey orders. That night I strained the muddy, foul water of the run through a blanket to get water to make coffee and to fill my canteen. We were almost out of food. I was entirely so.

On the morning of June 15th we moved close to the James River and parked. I was lying under a tree near an old and abandoned house. Below me and a little to my left a pontoon bridge stretched across the muddy waters of the river James. A few steamboats were paddling to and fro, some ferrying troops across the river, others apparently doing nothing. The Second Corps troops were rapidly marching across the pontoon bridge, which swayed up and down under their heavy tread. On the other side was a village of tents and great piles of boxes. Many men were swimming in the river.

I had had no supper, no breakfast, and I was

exceedingly hungry. One of my comrades and I were dolefully discussing the emptiness of our stomachs, when we saw an old, gray-haired negro walking past us. His tattered shirt was open at the breast, displaying a coat of moss-like, gray hair. His feet were bare. One of his hands grasped a cane, made of a piece of hickory sapling with prominent knobs on it, to help his legs support his withered old body. In his other hand he carried an aged and battered, but bright, tin pail. I hailed him, saying: "Uncle, come here." He stood in front of us, with water running out of his bleary eyes. He was exceedingly old and feeble. I said: "Uncle, we are hungry. There is a safeguard on those buildings," indicating a group of houses with outstretched arm, "and we cannot plunder them. Can you get us something to eat?" The old negro looked doubtfully from my comrade to me, and then back to my comrade. He hesitated to offer us what he had. Then he lifted the lid of his pail and dropped his long, lean, withered hand into it and drew forth a hoe-cake—a thick, brown hoe-cake—and handed it to me. I was ashamed to take it. But the old slave assured me that he had a store of meal laid by, and that he would not suffer.

So I took it and divided it with my comrade. The aged negro hobbled off to his work dinnerless.

Infantry hurried past us; batteries of artillery rolled by. We recognized some of the latter, and said: " There goes K. of the Fourth United States Artillery "; " That is the Twelfth New York Battery," and we waved our hands to the men whom we knew. There was a gap in the column of hurrying troops. Our captain swung himself into his saddle and commanded: " By piece from the right front into column, march!" and we were off for Petersburg. We crossed on the pontoon bridge, which had a peculiar earthquaky motion, and entered the village of tents. Thousands of boxes of hard bread and barrels of pork were there, but instead of being open and we helping ourselves as we marched, the troops were halted and jammed and irritated by having to stand around with open haversacks while a comparatively few commissary employees slowly dealt out the precious provisions to us. Hours were worth millions of dollars each on this flank movement. They were really priceless, and we dawdled away three of them in getting a little food into our haversacks. This was Potomac

Army economy. The Second Corps, if the boxes of hard bread and barrels of pork and coffee and sugar had lined the road, and we enlisted men had helped ourselves, might have carried off $20,000 worth of extra provisions; but we would have saved three hours, and they, if properly used, would have been worth $100,-000,000 each, and would ·have saved thousands of men's lives also. But we fooled away the time; we stood and chaffed one another; and the cannon in our front roared and the musketry rolled. Then we marched. We were in high spirits. We marched free. Every enlisted man in the Second Corps knew that we had outmarched the Confederates. We knew that some of our troops were assaulting the Confederate works at Petersburg. The booming of the cannon cheered us. We were tired, hungry, worn with six weeks of continuous and bloody fighting and severe marching; but now that we, the enlisted men of the Second Corps, knew that at last a flank movement had been successful, we wanted to push on and get into the fight and capture Petersburg. We knew that we had outmarched Lee's veterans, and that our reward was at hand. The Second Corps was in fine fettle, On all sides I heard men assert that Petersburg and Richmond were ours ; that the war would virtually be ended in less than twenty-four hours.

Night came. The almost full moon arose above the woods and gold-flecked the dust column which rose above us. We had heard heavy firing about sundown, and judged that we should be drawing near the battle-line. We entered a pine woods, and there we met a mob of black troops, who were hauling some brass guns. They had attached long ropes to the limbers, and, with many shouts, were dragging them down the road. Some of them bore flaming torches of pine knots in their hands. They sang, they shouted, they danced weirdly, as though they were again in Congo villages making medicine. They were happy, dirty, savagely excited, but they were not soldiers. As we, the Second Corps, met these victorious troops the eager infantrymen asked : " Where did you get those guns ? " They replied : " We'uns captured them from the rebels to-day." " Bah ! " an infantry sergeant, who was marching by my side, exclaimed, " you negroes captured nothing from Lee's men. The city is ours. There is not a brigade of the Army of Northern Virginia ahead of us." And we all exclaimed : " The city is ours ! We have out-marched them ! " And we strode on through the dense dust clouds, with parched throats, footsore and weary. Not a grumble did I hear. But with set jaws we toiled on, intent on capturing Petersburg before the Army of Northern Virginia got behind the works. It was " March, march, march ! No straggling now. It is far better to march to-night than to assault earthworks defended by Lee's men to-morrow. Hurry along ! hurry, hurry, hurry ! " And we marched our best. We passed a group of soldiers, who wore the distinctive badge of the Second Corps, cooking by the roadside, their muskets stacked by their fire. We asked how far it was to the battle-line. " Only a few hundred yards," they replied. Then we asked what Confederate troops were ahead of us. They answered, with a scornful laugh : " Petersburg militia." We asked what Union troops were engaged, and they replied : " Some of Butler's men." With the dislike all soldiers have for unknown troops, we said heartily : " Damn Butler's men ! We do not know them. We wish the Fifth or the Sixth Corps were here instead of them." Many soldiers anxiously inquired : " Will Butler's men fight ? " Then some private, who was better informed than the most of us, told us that Butler's men had been lying at Bermuda Hundreds, and that there were many negro troops among them. The noses of the Second Corps men were cocked sharply in the air at this information.

Word was passed among us that the negro troops had had famous success that day ; that they had wrested a heavy line of earthworks from the Confederates, and had captured eighteen guns. The soldiers halted for an instant. They examined their rifles and shifted their cartridge-boxes to a position where they could get at them easily, and they drank deeply from their canteens. Then belts were tightened, blanket rolls shifted, the last bits of hard-tack the men had been chewing were swallowed, and their mouths again filled with water and rinsed out, and then throughout the ranks murmurs arose of : " Now for it "; " Put us into it, Hancock, my boy; we will end this damned rebellion to-night!" and we laughed lowly, and our hearts beat high. Soon we heard commands given to the infantry, and they marched off. My battery moved forward, twisted obliquely in and out among the stumps, and then the guns swung into battery on a cleared space.

And then—and then—we went to cooking. That night was made to fight on. A bright and almost full moon shone above us. The Confederate earthworks were in plain view before us, earthworks which we knew were bare of soldiers. There was a noisy fire from the Confederate pickets in front of us. So unnerved and frightened were they that their bullets sang high above us. We cooked and ate, and fooled the time away. This when every intelligent enlisted man in the Second Corps knew that not many miles away the columns of the Army of Northern Virginia were marching furiously to save Petersburg and Richmond and the Confederacy. We could almost see those veteran troops, lean, squalid, hungry and battle torn, with set jaws and anxious-looking eyes, striding rapidly through the dust, pouring over bridges, crowding through the streets of villages, and ever hurrying on to face us. And we knew that once they got behind the earthworks in our front, we could not drive them out. They did not surrender cannon and intrenchments to disorderly gangs of armed negroes. They did not understand how troops could lose earthworks when assailed by equal numbers of soldiers. Still we cooked and ate, and sat idly look-

ing into one anothers eyes, questioningly at first,
then impatiently and then angrily.   Gradually
the fact that we were not to fight that night impressed itself on us.   I walked over to the limber of my gun, opened my knapsack, and took
out a campaign map and a pair of compasses.
Returning to the fire the map was spread on the
ground.   As I measured the distances a group
of excited soldiers gathered around and watched the work.   We had the less distance to
march, about nine hours' the start, and allowing
for the time lost at the crossing of the James
River we were at 11 P.M. four or five hours a-
head of the Army of Northern Virginia. "Will
they be in the works by morning, men?" I
asked ; and all answered, "By God, they will ! "
Discouraged, I put away the map, loaded a pipe,
lighted it, and strolled off down the line, stopping at almost every fire I came to to talk to
the infantry soldiers.   The rage of the intelligent enlisted men was devilish.   The most
blood-curdling blasphemy I ever listened to I
heard that night, uttered by the men who knew
they were to be sacrificed on the morrow.   The
whole corps was furiously excited.   I returned
to my battery a little after midnight.   Seated
on the ground I rested my back against one of

the ponderous wheels of my gun. Resting there I slept.

At early dawn I was awake and tried to examine the Confederate line. I noticed that the noisy, wasteful picket-firing of the night before had ceased; that the main line of earthworks, indistinctly seen in the gray light, was silent. Some of our infantry came into our slight earthwork, and we stood gazing into the indistinctness before us. All of us were greatly depressed.

It grew lighter and lighter, and there before us, fully revealed, was a long, high line of intrenchments, with heavy redoubts, where cannon were massed at the angles, silent, grim. No wasteful fire shot forth from that line. Now and then a man rose up out of the Confederate rifle-pits, and a rifle-ball flew close above us, no longer singing high in the air. Sadly we looked at one another. We knew that the men who had fought us in the Wilderness, at Spottsylvania, North Anna, and Cold Harbor were in the works sleeping, gaining strength to repulse our assault, while their pickets watched for them.

No one has ever accused General Hancock of lying.

It was broad daylight. I had eaten my

breakfast and was looking over the field of yesterday's fighting. Some dead men lay on the ground; but the scarcity of those in gray plainly showed that they had no stomach for fighting, that they were raw, undisciplined militia, who had abandoned their powerful line of earthworks when attacked by a few black troops. At sixty feet in front of the captured works I saw pine trees which had been struck with Confederate bullets thirty feet from the ground. This told, better than words, the nervous condition of the men who pretended to defend the line.

Wandering toward the rear, I came on the line of rifle-pits which had been used by the Confederate pickets, and saw two dead men lying close together. I walked over to them. One was a burly negro sergeant, as black as coal, in blue; the other was a Confederate line sergeant, in gray. Their bayoneted rifles lay beside them. Curious at the nearness of the bodies, I turned them over and looked carefully at them. They had met with unloaded rifles and had fought a duel with their bayonets, each stabbing the other to death.

The battery bugler blew "boots and saddles!" and I hastened back to my gun, to hear that the other corps of the Potomac Army had arrived, and that the infantry would make a general assault that day, probably in the after-noon. We limbered up; then marched to the left and took a new position on a bit of level land which gradually sloped toward a creek which flowed between us and the silent Confed-erate line. The preliminary artillery practice began, so as to announce in thunder tones that we were getting ready to make an assault. I worked listlessly to and fro from the muzzle of my three-inch gun, carelessly looking ahead to see if the fire produced any result. It did not. The gunners of the Confederate batteries were evidently husbanding their ammunition. They treated us with silent contempt. But, unable to withstand our steady hammering, they at last coldly responded to our attentions. Shot skipped by us, shell exploded among us; but, with very unusual luck, we lost but few men.

We fired steadily. The limber of the gun was emptied. It went back to the line of caissons to be filled and the limber of the cais-sons came up. Soon the operation was re-peated and I knew that the caissons would speedily go to the rear after ammunition. After a little while the first sergeant came to me and

said : " You seem to be tired.   Go to the rear
with the caissons after ammunition." I handed
the heavy sponge staff to another cannoneer
and walked to the caissons.   Mounting on the
empty chests I rode to the rear where the
ammunition wagons were parked.   A portion
of the road we travelled over ran within three
fourths of a mile of a heavy Confederate redoubt, out of whose embrasures the muzzles of
large black guns were thrust.   To the right of
this piece of road was an open field of thin,
poverty-creating soil ; beyond the field was
a forest.   Thickly scattered among the trees,
and grouped at the edge of the open field, in
the shade, were those cowards, the " coffee
boilers."   Gangs of officers' servants and many
refugee negroes were there. Pack-mules loaded
with pots, frying-pans, gripsacks, and bags of
clothing stood tied to trees.   White-capped
army wagons, with six mules harnessed to them,
stood at the edge of the woods.   The drivers
of these wagons were drinking coffee with
friendly " boilers," and they were probably
frightening one another by telling blood-curdling tales of desperate but mythical battles
they had been engaged in.   Fires were burning
brightly in the forest, and thin columns of

smoke arose above the trees. I could almost smell the freshly made Rio and the broiled bacon. It was as though a huge pic-nic were going on in the woods. The scene angered me. I knew that the "coffee boilers" were almost to a man bounty-jumping cowards, and I wanted that camp broken up.

The Confederates in the redoubt allowed us to pass to the rear without firing on us; for we were empty and not worth powder and shot. Arriving at the park of the ammunition train we filled our ammunition chests, and then began the return march. When the full caissons came out of the woods on to the portion of the road which was exposed to the fire from the fort, I saw the Confederate gunners spring to their cannon. I looked at the camp of the "coffee boilers." They were enjoying life. I leaned forward and clasped my knees with excess of joy as I realized what was about to occur. The Confederate gunners were going to try to blow up our caissons. I was confident that they could not hit us, and was also confident that their attempt would bloodily disturb the camp of the "boilers" and hangers-on. We broke into a trot, then into a gallop, and then into a dead run. Clouds of smoke shot forth

from the redoubt, and out of these, large black
balls rose upward and rushed through the air,
and passed, shrieking shrilly, close above us,
to descend in the camp of the "boilers." It
was a delightful scene. I hugged my knees and
rocked to and fro and laughed until my fleshless ribs were sore. Shells swept above me and
burst in the woods. Shot howled past and cut
large trees down, and they fell with a crash
among the frying-pans and coffee-pots. Team-
sters sprang into their wagons, or on to their
saddle-mules, and savagely plied their whips
and hastened away from the pasture-field.
Negro servants loosened their pack-mules and
hung on to the loads of tinware as they, yelling
at the top of their voices, ran for the rear.
Men, clad and armed as soldiers, skurried as
frightened rabbits, hid in holes, lay prone on
the earth, dropped behind logs. Through the
dust and smoke and uproar I saw men fall,
saw others mangled by chunks of shell, and saw
one, struck fairly by an exploding shell, vanish.
Enormously pleased, I hugged my lean legs,
and laughed and laughed again. It was the
most refreshing sight I had seen for weeks.
Our caissons, each drawn by six galloping
horses, passed safely through the fire and

entered the protective woods, and, moving rapidly across the blood-chilling belt where the spent balls fall and the wounded lie, were soon on the battle line, and I was again engaged in helping to waste good powder and shot and shell.

The afternoon passed quickly away. One of the caissons, which belonged to a battery that was in action alongside of us, struck by a shell, blew up, and two men were blown up with it. A long bolt made by our English brothers, did this work, and it added to my dislike of all things English. As the sun sank the infantry prepared to deliver the assault that we had been announcing as to be made. A staff officer rode up ; we ceased firing. The smoke drifted off of the field. Utterly exhausted, I threw myself on the hot ground and watched the doomed men who were to try to carry the Confederate line. The charging cheer rang out loudly, the line of blue-clad soldiers rushed forward, the Confederate pickets emptied their rifles, jumped from their rifle-pits, and ran for their main line, which was still silent excepting the artillery. This was served rapidly, but not very effectively. The line of blue swept on in good order, cheering loudly and continuously.

They drew near to the Confederate earthworks. Canister cut gaps in the ranks. Then the heads of Lee's infantry rose above their intrenchments. I saw the glint of the sun on their polished rifle barrels. A cloud of smoke curled along the works. Our men began to tumble in large numbers; some fell forward, others backward, others staggered a few steps and then sank down as though to rest. Still I did not hear the roll of the musketry. Suddenly it burst on me, mingled with the fierce Confederate battle-cry. The field grew hazy with smoke. Rifles were tossed high in the air. Battle flags went down with a sweep, to again appear and plunge into the smoke. Wounded men straggled out of the battle. Fresh troops hurried by the battery and disappeared in the hazy smoke. Away off to our right I heard the charging cheer of our soldiers and the thunderous roll of musketry; to the left more musketry and exultant howls, as though we had met with success. In our front the fire grew steadily fiercer and fiercer. The wounded men, who drifted through the battery, told us that the works were very strong, and that beyond them there was another and still stronger line, and that our troops were fighting in the open before the front line and were not meeting with any success. Night settled down, and the fight still went on ; but it fagged. The musketry was no longer a steady roar, and we could see the flashes of the rifles, and the Confederate parapet glowing redly. At points the musketry fire broke out fiercely, then died down. In our front the fight was over. My battery moved forward under the direction of a staff officer, and we threw up an earthwork.

That night the news gatherers walked the battle lines. They told us that the assault had been bloodily repulsed excepting at one or two unimportant points. And they also brought an exceedingly interesting bit of news or gossip, or a camp rumor. They said : " We have heard from some of Butler's men that in the breast pocket of the coat of a Confederate officer, who was killed in front of their lines at Bermuda Hundreds on June 15th, was found the 'morning report ' of the Confederate army which was defending Petersburg on that day, and that this report showed that Beauregard did not have over 10,000 men, most of whom were militia, with which to defend Petersburg, and that Butler had laid this report before Baldy Smith and Hancock, and had urged them to make the assault and capture Petersburg before the Army of Northern Virginia came up ; but that they, Smith and Hancock, had hesitated and dawdled the night away."

In the morning I saw that there had been some advance of the line. The Second Corps had gained a little ground at great cost, and we heard that Burnside had also gained ground and captured a redoubt. The dead soldiers of the Second Corps lay thickly in front of us, placed in long trenches by their comrades.

That afternoon the battery quartermaster-sergeant, goaded to desperation by the taunts of the artillery privates, nerved himself with whiskey and came to the battery to display his courage. The Confederate sharp-shooters had attacked us about noon, and our works were hot. I, snugly seated under the earthworks, looked at this representative of the staff with all the intense dislike privates have for the gold-laced officers. I was wicked enough to wish that he would get shot. He swaggered up and down behind the guns, talking loudly, and ignorant of the danger. I, with high-beating heart, looked eagerly at him, hungrily waiting for him to jump and howl. I was disappointed. A sharp-shooter's bullet struck him on the throat. It crashed through his spine at the base of the brain, and he neither jumped nor howled—simply fell on his back dead.

Early on the morning of June 18th, some of our pickets brought word to the battery that the Confederates had abandoned their front line during the night, and that they had moved back to their interior line, which was shorter and stronger and more easily defended. The infantry soldiers moved forward, and occupied the works they had been unable to capture. My battery moved to another position, and again the guns opened on the Confederate line, and again they husbanded their ammunition. But their sharp-shooters fairly made us howl with anguish. I heartily wished that Lee had not abandoned his front line. Our infantry moved to and fro, getting ready to assault the new line of intrenchments. The soldiers were thoroughly discouraged. They had no heart for the assault. It was evident that they had determined not to fight stanchly, not to attempt to accomplish the impossible. At about four o'clock in the afternoon the infantry was sent to the slaughter, and the Confederates promptly killed a sufficient number of them to satisfy our generals that the works could not be taken by assaults delivered by exhausted and discouraged troops. In many places our battle line did not advance to the line of rifle-pits held by the Confederate pickets. We had lost about 12,000 men in the attempts to capture Petersburg. The Second Corps could have taken the city on the night of June 15th without losing more than 500 men. This fact disheartened the enlisted men of the Army of the Potomac. They were supremely disgusted with the display of military stupidity our generals had made.

We marched somewhere at night. The road was lined with sleeping infantry. I was hungry. As I look back at those bloody days it seems to me that I was always hungry. Men to the right of us, to the left of us, lay as though dead—they slept so soundly ; but their haversacks were not in sight. They were veterans who knew enough to hide their haversacks when they slept on roads. We came to a heavy double line of men, who looked as if they had opened ranks and then fallen over asleep. Soon we light-artillery men recognized them as 100-day men from Ohio. Their haversacks stood at their heads. Wickedly we all went to plundering the 100-day men as they slept. We exchanged our empty haversacks for full ones, and every man of us had a spare haversack filled with food hanging on the guns or caissons. At the time I thought it a capital joke on the Ohio men; but I now think that some of those men were very hungry before they got any thing to eat. They must have bitter recollections of the night march of some of the Second Corps' artillery.

In the morning we marched over ground where there had been fighting the evening before. Sitting at the base of a pine tree I saw a line sergeant. His face was stained with blood, which had oozed from under a bandage made of an old shirt sleeve, tightly bound around his eyes. By his side sat a little drummer boy, with unstrung drum and the sticks put up standing on the ground before him. The muscular form of the sergeant was bent forward, his chin resting on his hands, his elbows on his knees. His figure conveyed to me the impression of utter hopelessness. The small drummer looked up the road, and then down the road, with anxious gaze. I stopped for an instant, and asked, "What is the matter?" The drummer looked up at me, his blue eyes filled with tears, and answered: "He 's my

father. Both his eyes were blinded on the
picket line this morning. I am waiting for an
ambulance to come along. I don't know where
the field hospitals are." I hurriedly pointed in
the direction of some field hospitals we had
passed a few hundred yards back. The two
rose up and walked slowly off, the son leading
his blinded father by the hand, leading him to
the operating-table, and I hastened on, swallow-
ing my tears and cursing the delay to take
Petersburg.

Some stragglers, bearing the red cross on
their caps, were passed, and we were satisfied
that we were not merely changing position,
but that we were on the flanking move again.
We got into a thickly wooded country, and,
without a particle of warning, the men in gray
burst from cover and were on us. There was
some exceedingly severe fighting here, and we
got decidedly the worst of it, being driven
back beyond the Jerusalem plank-road in great
disorder. A group of artillerymen, some of
them wounded, came down the line and dropped
into our battery. They told us that their battery had been captured, and that the infantry
who fought near their guns had lost severely,
many prisoners being taken by the Confeder-

ates ; but that when they left, our troops were holding their ground, and had connected with the Sixth Corps. We held the ground we were fighting on, slept on it, and the next morning again pushed on in column, to be again savagely attacked on our flank by heavy masses of Confederate infantry in column. Again we were roughly handled, losing more guns and many prisoners. The country was so densely wooded that I could see but little of this fighting. I simply served my gun, and looked ahead into the forest, expecting to be hit by a rifle-ball at any instant. Next morning we pushed on again, having driven the Confederates off during the night, and soon reached the Weldon Railroad. There we got soundly thrashed and gladly retreated, having lost more guns and many more prisoners.

I talked to some rebel prisoners and swapped food for tobacco. They told me that it was Hill's Corps which had been so persistently attentive to us. They were inclined to boast about one of their corps handling two of our crack corps. In truth they had torn us badly. One long-legged, dangling Cracker, with a broad, derisive grin on his face, which displayed his long, tobacco-stained teeth, said to me, drawlingly : " Say, sonny, did you clover-leaf chaps get a bellyful?" I assured him we had room for more, whereat he grinned and marched to the rear with his comrades.

I had had enough of marching and fighting— enough of seeing good men's lives squandered in assaults against earthworks. The continuous strain was greater than the soldiers, poorly fed and exposed to the weather (the enlisted men had no tents during this bloody and wasteful campaign), could bear. As I have said, I got heartsick and weary of the fighting, and believed that Grant could not capture Petersburg until he had disciplined his army, which would take months, as by far the larger portion of the troops were new to the field, and were bounty-paid recruits. About 70,000 of the good men we had crossed the Rapidan with lay dead behind us, or were in hospitals, or languished in Confederate military prisons. So I, one morning, claimed my discharge, which had been ordered by Secretary of War Stanton while we were fighting in front of Cold Harbor. Getting it, I went to Washington, where a commission in the Fourth United States Artillery awaited me.

X.

CONDITION OF THE ARMY OF THE POTOMAC AFTER PETERSBURG.

THE memories of the war are growing dim. The ranks of the men who carried arms through Grant's last campaign are being thinned rapidly by death. In a few years all of us will join our comrades who fell dead along the bloody trail that led from the Wilderness thickets to the fair fields that surrounded the beleaguered cities of Petersburg and Richmond. If a truthful statement is to be made of the Army of the Potomac, of its *morale*, when the enlisted men sank exhausted into their trenches before Petersburg, it must be made quickly or not at all. I write this chapter after much consideration, and I write it solely in the interests of truth and to put permanently on record, so that future generations of Americans can read it, the opinions of many intelligent men who fought in the ranks throughout that bloody campaign.

Late in the afternoon of June 18, 1864, and

while the battery to which I belonged was actively shelling a Confederate earthwork, and getting shelled in return, a brigade of infantry passed close behind our guns. I was sick with a coming fever. I had exhausted my strength in the morning, and was serving at the caissons during the afternoon. The brigade of infantry passed within five yards of me. The infantry were weak and looked tired. Their steps were slow. The appearance of these troops attracted my attention. I saw that they were veterans, and greatly superior to the motley crew into which the Army of the Potomac had degenerated. The brigade was about 500 muskets strong. I spoke to one of the men, asking what command it was, and he answered, whether truthfully or not I cannot say, "The Excelsior Brigade of the Second Corps." That brigade was a fighting brigade, justly famed throughout the Army of the Potomac for their desperate valor. It was the peer of the famous brigades from Vermont and New Hampshire.

"Going in to the charge, men?" I asked.

Nine or ten of the tired infantry soldiers heard the question, and they growled out an explanatory answer in tones that expressed the most profound disgust :

" No, we are not going to charge. We are going to run towards the Confederate earthworks, and then we are going to run back. We have had enough of assaulting earthworks. We are hungry and tired, and we want to rest and to eat."

I spoke to other men farther down the short column, and, in effect, received the same answer. I went to the rear after ammunition that afternoon, and I met other troops going to the front. I spoke to many of these men, and all I spoke to were resolute in their purpose not to make a determined charge of the Confederate intrenchments. And they did not.

At the time, in the latter part of June, 1864, it was freely charged by the generals employed in the Army of the Potomac that the army was not fighting as stanchly at Petersburg as it had fought in the Wilderness or at Spottsylvania. The charge was true. But was it the enlisted men alone who shrank from the bloody work of assaulting earthworks behind which the clear-eyed, nervy, veteran Confederate infantry lurked? Let the figures, presumably official, as published in the work entitled " Grant and his Campaigns," speak in answer, and it must be borne in mind that these figures were never accepted by the enlisted men as truthfully representing their losses during the campaign. We had seen regiments melt before the heat of the Confederate fire, until a scant hundred men fell into line when the drum tapped. We had seen brigades fall into battle line three hundred muskets strong. Once at Cold Harbor two regiments were sent to support my battery. I smiled sorrowfully at the scanty array. One hundred and twenty muskets, sixty files, were all that were left of two Delaware regiments. We had seen heavy-artillery regiments, which joined us at Spottsylvania, 1,500, 1,600, 1,700 men 'strong, fall into line before Petersburg 400, 500, 600 men strong, and to come back from the assault delivered on June 18, 1864, still weaker. The enlisted men who passed unharmed through the frightful carnage, judged the losses the army suffered by the actual losses that had occurred in regiments with which we were familiar.

To the official figures. During May, 1864, which period of time includes the prolonged study of Confederate intrenchments at North Anna, the Army of the Potomac lost 395 officers killed, 1,343 wounded, and 211 missing. Five or six general officers were killed and ten or twelve wounded during the month. In the same month 5,189 enlisted men were killed, 27,140 wounded, and 7,239 were missing. From May 31st to Oct. 28th, the day on which the campaign practically ended, in the Potomac Army 401 officers were killed, 1,453 wounded, and 564 missing; during the same time 4,587 enlisted men were killed, 24,110 were wounded, and 15,844 were missing. The aggregate losses after the fighting at North Anna were 46,989 enlisted men and officers. And the enlisted men never heard of but one general officer being killed. He was Brigadier-General Burnham. They heard of three or four other generals being wounded, and of two being captured. During this same time—that is, after the battle of North Anna—we learned from prisoners that the Confederate Generals Doles, Chambliss, Gherardio, Dunnovan, and Gregg had been killed, and many of their generals wounded. And it must be remembered that the Confederate generals were behind sheltering earthworks with their troops. The execution of their duty made it essential that they should be there. Our losses of general officers, if they had fearlessly performed their duty, should have been at least four times as heavy as those of the Confederates.   Instead of one Union general being killed to over 44,000 enlisted men stricken in battle, there should have been at least twenty of them killed and eighty of them wounded, and there probably would have been if they had done their duty as recklessly as the Confederate generals did theirs. Let me go west, and to the battle of Franklin, to illustrate my meaning.   On the afternoon of November 30, 1864, the Confederate generals led their veteran infantry to the assault against the hastily constructed Union earthworks, thrown up across a broad neck of land formed by a bend in the Harpeth River, in Tennessee. The attack began at 4 P.M.   It was dark at 6 P.M.   The fight lasted until about 10 P.M.   Say six hours of fighting, four of which were performed after dark, when it was impossible for infantry to select generals as targets, or to shoot accurately.   The Confederates lost about 6,000 enlisted men in this action, and four Confederate generals were killed and six so severely wounded that they left the front.   In truth, every general in the Confederate army which fought at Franklin, excepting General Hood, was either killed or wounded.   So fought the Confederate leaders in the field.   So Southern generals led their soldiers to death and shared it with them.

It is true the regulars, typified by Major-General Griffin of the Fifth Corps, and volunteers by Major-General Francis C. Barlow of the Second Corps, commanded the universal respect of the enlisted men. We knew the fighting generals and we respected them, and we knew the cowards and despised them.

It was frequently and truthfully asserted that the Army of the Potomac did not fight as steadily and persistently around Petersburg as it had done in the Wilderness and around Spottsylvania. In other words, that the great army had become demoralized. I believe that the demoralization of the Army of the Potomac was due to two causes, which were at that time fully understood by all the intelligent volunteers in the army. The first and minor cause was the shirking of bloody work by some of the generals, which disheartened the enlisted men and imbittered them.

The second and potent cause of the demoralization of the Army of the Potomac was the worthless character of the recruits who were supplied to the army in 1864–65, In 1864 requisitions calling for 500,000 troops were

made on the North.   So thoroughly exhausted
was the breed of fighting men in the North
that but 169,000 of the enormous number of
men raised by purchase ever stood in battle
ranks, and they stood there because they had
been unable to elude the vigilance or corrupt
the honesty of the guards who accompanied
them from the recruiting barracks to the front.
Since man has been on earth the race has been
divided into classes, one of which is the criminal class.   This class live by plundering the
producing class.   They live by theft, by murder, by cheating, by pandering to the ignoble
vices of men.   When the Northern townships
began to pay bounties for recruits to fill the
quotas allotted to them, the criminal class of
America quit preying on society at large, and
turned their attention to swindling the government.   They accepted the bounty offered by
the towns and enlisted.   When the bounties
were paid to them they deserted and enlisted
in another town, to again desert.   Bounty-
jumping was the safest and most profitable
business in the United States during those
days.   The boldest and most intelligent of the
criminal class never appeared at the front.
They escaped.   The weak, the diseased, the

feeble-minded joined the army. They were the scum of the slums of the great European and American cities. To these were added the rakings of rural almshouses and the never-do-wells of villages. The recruits were faint-hearted and stupid. Many were irreclaimable blackguards, wholly given over to numerous ignoble and unnamable vices. They were moral lepers. They were conscienceless, cowardly scoundrels, and the clean-minded American and Irish and German volunteers would not associate with them.

Directly after the battle of Cold Harbor these pretended soldiers began to be noticeable in the Army of the Potomac. They were not the heavy-artillery men drawn by Grant from Washington to make good his losses. We had no better troops than those. But these men were the bounty-paid substitutes. They were the white slaves, whom greedy and unpatriotic men, who preyed on the necessities of timid communities, gathered from the slums, from Castle Garden, from the almshouses, from the cots of venereal hospitals, from the bars of criminal courts, from prison cells, and from the unnatural parents of weak-minded sons. After gathering the foul creatures, they kept them in pens and private prisons. Over the doors of these dens swung signs, and blazoned on them in gilt letters were shameful legends which announced that within a man dealt in alleged men, and that the honor of townships could be pawned there. A Mississippi slave-dealer was a refined and honorable gentleman in comparison with a Northern bounty-broker, who sold men to the townships which filled their quotas by purchase. I have seen these substitutes, many of them unable to speak English, vermin infested, rough-skinned, stinking with disease, their eyes running matter, their legs and arms thin and feeble, their backs bowed, and their rat-like and idiot-like heads hanging low, join the army to be virtually kicked out of the decent commands they were billeted on. They were scorned, kicked, and cursed by the volunteers as mangy curs. These degraded men formed the " coffee boilers."

I first saw systematic " coffee boiling," a sure sign that discipline was relaxed, at Cold Harbor. In the woods to the rear and right of my battery, groups of unwounded men cooked and boiled coffee. These men had dropped out of their commands as they approached the battle line, and had hidden in the woods. There were hundreds of them in the army at Cold Harbor. There were hundreds of them around Petersburg. They sneaked away from their regiments during battle, or while marching to battle, to rejoin them when on the march. They were always present when rations were issued. They were never present when cartridges were supplied. They were, without exception, thieves. They robbed the dead. They stole from the living. They were strongly suspected of killing wounded men at night. More cowardly creatures were never clad in the uniform of English-speaking peoples. They plundered houses. They frightened women and little children. They burned dwellings. To call a soldier of the Army of the Potomac a " coffee boiler " was an insult to be promptly resented.

These worthless creatures weakened every battle line they were forced into. No matter how brave a veteran soldier may be, he relies on the men on either side of him to stand there until they fall. He relies on them to accompany him in the advance, and to be by his side when slowly falling back before a superior force. It is essential that a soldier hears the voices of his comrades when he is charging. He must know that his comrades are as stanch fighters as he. Then he can fight with comparative comfort. How was it with the larger portions of the bounty-paid recruits raised in 1864? It did not lie within the power of any regimental officers to hold these undisciplined blackguards steady under fire. Dozens of times I have seen them break and run, throwing away their arms as they fled, yelling, to the rear and to their coffee-pots. They weakened the battle lines, as no man can fight when surrounded by cowards, who are easily panic-stricken, and who are unrestrained by any consideration of pride from ignominiously running away to save their lives. No man really enjoys a battle. One has to string up his nerves and take a firm grip on himself morally, and hold himself in the battle flames for a few moments until warmed to passion. The impulse is to run out of the danger. The men the bounty-brokers supplied to the army had no morality, no sentiment except of fear, and they could not and would not stand fire. They desired to live to enjoy the spending of the money they had received. So they shirked, and ran, and boiled coffee in the rear until gathered up by the provost guards and sent to their regiments. They were disciplined somewhat during the winter of

1864–65. Previous to the spring of 1865 the larger portion of the bounty-paid recruits would not have been worth burning Confederate powder to kill, as their presence in our ranks impaired the efficiency of our army. They could have been safely killed with clubs.

After the battle of June 18, 1864, the enlisted men frequently discussed the condition of the Army of the Potomac. They sat o' nights in groups behind the intrenchments and talked, talked, talked of the disintegrating force which Grant commanded. Enormous losses of prisoners were reported, losses that were incurred while charging earthworks, which fact clearly showed that our troops had surrendered after reaching the Confederate intrenchments — surrendered rather than attempt to take them or to return to our line under the deadly accurate fire of the Confederate infantry. Many of the volunteers vehemently asserted that the bounty-paid recruits really deserted during action to seek safety in Confederate prison pens. The enlisted men who had gathered into ranks under McClellan, and who had been forged into soldiers by that admirable drill-master, all said that the Army of the Potomac of 1862 was far superior, man to man, to that which crossed

the Rapidan in May of 1864, and immeasur-
ably superior to the army which lay in the
trenches before Petersburg in July of 1864.
They also asserted, and truthfully, that if the
original volunteers, or men as good as they
were, were commanded by Grant he would
capture Richmond in twenty-four hours.   The
enlisted men spent much time in comparing
Grant with McClellan.   The latter had many
warm friends among the soldiers.   He only of
all the men who had commanded the Army of
the Potomac was personally liked and admired
by his troops.   Soldiers' eyes would brighten
when they talked of him.   Their hard, lean,
browned faces would soften and light up with
affection when they spoke of him,—and still it
was affection only; they did not, as a rule, con-
cede to him military talent.   And the general
opinion among them was; given Grant in command of the army in 1862, and the rebellion
would have been crushed that year.   Asked
how McClellan would have done with the army
of 1864 under his command, they shrugged
their shoulders and said dryly: "Well, he
would have ended the war in the Wilderness—
by establishing the Confederacy."

One night as we sat around the guns talking

with visitors from a New Hampshire regiment, a private, young in years, but old in service, said :

"McClellan expected American volunteers to fight day after day. Outfought and beaten to-day, they must fight to-morrow as though ever victorious, and they did it when he commanded them. He taught us to fight, and all that is good in this many-tongued crew of Grant's, the leaven of it, is the remnant of McClellan's army. Grant has not moulded one man in this vast mob. He has filled our ranks as best he could, but he depends on the men who sprang to arms when the Northern war-drum sounded, to supply these bounty-jumping recruits with courage and to teach them their duty. Take the volunteers away from the Army of the Potomac, and Lee could drown the rest of this army in the James River without firing a shot."

"Drown them!" exclaimed a young soldier who was raised on the shores of Sunapee Lake in New Hampshire. "Drown them! Curse them! I am afraid to fight with any of them standing by my side. There is a man from Manchester, who was paid $1,000 for enlisting, whose place in line is next to me. It keeps me busy to hold him from running away

whenever we are under fire. Some day he will
be so badly frightened that he will run toward
the Confederates instead of away from them,
and then I am going to kill him. If ever he
gets a little ahead of me, so that I can safely
kill him, I will gather him in." No one seemed
to be shocked at his intention. "Drown
them?" he scornfully repeated; "Lee's veterans drown them? Yes, they could push
them into the James River with pine poles,
and as they sank they would howl for mercy
in twenty-seven languages. See here, men," he
added, impressively, "if Grant ever intends to
take yonder earthworks," jerking his thumb
over his shoulder to indicate the Confederate
lines, "he has got to give these bounty-jumpers
about six months of steady drilling, six months
of severe discipline, six months of punishment
and savage abuse. They have got to be pounded and hammered until they are in abject fear
of their line officers and are taught that to
shrink means death. If Grant gives them that,
they can be made to fight next spring. Good
God, men!" he exclaimed, "I was sent to City
Point the other day, and I passed a short column
of troops who were moving to the front, and I
saw dozens of the men fall out and endeavor

to hide in the brush and woods. Behind the column came a detachment of the provost guards, and these soldiers had to pick up and head off and surround the abject wretches who sought to hide long before they were within sight of the line of fire. They were panic-stricken at the prospect of fighting. They had to be prodded with bayonets to make them follow the column. Things have come to a pretty pass in this army if a column of troops cannot be moved from one camp to another without being herded as sheep driven along a highway! American volunteers!" he scornfully exclaimed; "American volunteers, and marched to camp or to battle under provost guards! They are not Americans, they are not volunteers: they are the offscouring of Europe. They disgrace our uniform." Here his scorn overcame him. He spat on the ground, arose and disappeared in the forest with a yell of disgust. And I knew that every word he had uttered was true.

Throughout the latter portion of the campaign the enlisted men, the volunteers, complained bitterly of the lack of judgment displayed by some of the commanding officers, and as freely as I talked with my comrades, as dirty, vermin-infested, and hungry we sat behind our earthworks, so freely do I claim the right to write now. I have faithfully endeavored to tell how the enlisted men, who put down the slaveholders' rebellion, felt and talked and lived in hopes long deferred and never fulfilled, of the coming of a great commander whose military talent would command our unqualified respect. He never came.

XI.

HOW MEN DIE IN BATTLE.

ALMOST every death on the battle-field is different. And the manner of the death depends on the wound and on the man, whether he is cowardly or brave, whether his vitality is large or small, whether he is a man of active imagination or is dull of intellect, whether he is of nervous or lymphatic temperament. I instance deaths and wounds that I saw in Grant's last campaign.

On the second day of the battle of the Wilderness, where I fought as an infantry soldier, I saw more men killed and wounded than I did before or after in the same time. I knew but few of the men in the regiment in whose ranks I stood; but I learned the Christian names of some of them. The man who stood next to me on my right was called Will. He was cool, brave, and intelligent. In the morning, when the Second Corps was advancing and driving Hill's soldiers slowly back, I was flurried. He noticed it, and steadied my nerves by saying, kindly : "Don't fire so fast. This fight will last all day. Don't hurry. Cover your man before you pull your trigger. Take it easy, my boy, take it easy, and your cartridges will last the longer." This man fought effectively. During the day I had learned to look up to this excellent soldier, and lean on him. Toward evening, as we were being slowly driven back to the Brock Road by Longstreet's men, we made a stand. I was behind a tree firing, with my rifle barrel resting on the stub of a limb. Will was standing by my side, but in the open. He, with a groan, doubled up and dropped on the ground at my feet. He looked up at me. His face was pale. He gasped for breath a few times, and then said, faintly : " That ends me. I am shot through the bowels." I said : "Crawl to the rear. We are not far from the intrench-ments along the Brock Road." I saw him sit up, and indistinctly saw him reach for his rifle, which had fallen from his hands as he fell. Again I spoke to him, urging him to go to the rear. He looked at me and said impatiently : " I tell you that I am as good as dead. There is no use in fooling with me. I shall stay here." Then he pitched forward dead, shot again and

through the head. We fell back before Longstreet's soldiers and left Will lying in a windrow
of dead men.

When we got into the Brock Road intrenchments, a man a few files to my left dropped
dead, shot just above the right eye. He did
not groan, or sigh, or make the slightest physical
movement, except that his chest heaved a few
times. The life went out of his face instantly,
leaving it without a particle of expression. It
was plastic, and, as the facial muscles contracted, it took many shapes. When this
man's body became cold, and his face hardened, it was horribly distorted, as though he
had suffered intensely. Any person who had
not seen him killed, would have said that he
had endured supreme agony before death released him. A few minutes after he fell, another man, a little farther to the left, fell with
apparently a precisely similar wound. He was
straightened out and lived for over an hour.
He did not speak. Simply lay on his back, and
his broad chest rose and fell, slowly at first,
and then faster and faster, and more and more
feebly, until he was dead. And his face hardened, and it was almost terrifying in its painful
distortion. I have seen dead soldiers' faces

which were wreathed in smiles, and heard their comrades say that they had died happy. I do not believe that the face of a dead soldier, lying on a battle-field, ever truthfully indicates the mental or physical anguish, or peacefulness of mind, which he suffered or enjoyed before his death. The face is plastic after death, and as the facial muscles cool and contract, they draw the face into many shapes. Sometimes the dead smile, again they stare with glassy eyes, and lolling tongues, and dreadfully distorted visages at you. It goes for nothing. One death was as painless as the other.

After Longstreet's soldiers had driven the Second Corps into their intrenchments along the Brock Road, a battle-exhausted infantry-man stood behind a large oak tree. His back rested against it. He was very tired, and held his rifle loosely in his hand. The Confederates were directly in our front. This soldier was apparently in perfect safety. A solid shot from a Confederate gun struck the oak tree squarely about four feet from the ground; but it did not have sufficient force to tear through the tough wood. The soldier fell dead. There was not a scratch on him. He was killed by concussion.

While we were fighting savagely over these intrenchments the woods in our front caught fire, and I saw many of our wounded burned to death.   Must they not have suffered horribly ? I am not at all sure of that.   The smoke rolled heavily and slowly before the fire.   It enveloped the wounded, and I think that by far the larger portion of the men who were roasted were suffocated before the flames curled round them. The spectacle was courage-sapping and pitiful, and it appealed strongly to the imagination of the spectators; but I do not believe that the wounded soldiers, who were being burned, suffered greatly, if they suffered at all.

Wounded soldiers, it mattered not how slight the wounds, generally hastened away from the battle lines.   A wound entitled a man to go to the rear and to a hospital.   Of course there were many exceptions to this rule, as there would necessarily be in battles where from twenty thousand to thirty thousand men were wounded.   I frequently saw slightly wounded men who were marching with their colors.   I personally saw but two men wounded who continued to fight.   During the first day's fighting in the wilderness I saw a youth of about twenty years skip and yell, stung by a

bullet through the thigh. He turned to limp
to the rear. After he had gone a few steps he
stopped, then he kicked out his leg once or
twice to see if it would work. Then he tore
the clothing away from his leg so as to see the
wound. He looked at it attentively for an instant, then kicked out his leg again, then turned
and took his place in the ranks and resumed
firing. There was considerable disorder in the
line, and the soldiers moved to and fro—now a
few feet to the right, now a few feet to the left.
One of these movements brought me directly
behind this wounded soldier. I could see
plainly from that position, and I pushed into
the gaping line and began firing. In a minute
or two the wounded soldier dropped his rifle,
and, clasping his left arm, exclaimed: " I am
hit again ! " He sat down behind the battle
ranks and tore off the sleeve of his shirt. The
wound was very slight—not much more than
skin deep. He tied his handkerchief around it,
picked up his rifle, and took position alongside
of me. I said : " You are fighting in bad luck
to-day. You had better get away from here."
He turned his head to answer me. His head
jerked, he staggered, then fell, then regained
his feet. A tiny fountain of blood and teeth

and bone and bits of tongue burst out of his mouth. He had been shot through the jaws; the lower one was broken and hung down. I looked directly into his open mouth, which was ragged and bloody and tongueless. He cast his rifle furiously on the ground and staggered off.

The next day, just before Longstreet's soldiers made their first charge on the Second Corps, I heard the peculiar cry a stricken man utters as the bullet tears through his flesh. I turned my head, as I loaded my rifle, to see who was hit. I saw a bearded Irishman pull up his shirt. He had been wounded in the left side just below the floating ribs. His face was gray with fear. The wound looked as though it were mortal. He looked at it for an instant, then poked it gently with his index finger. He flushed redly, and smiled with satisfaction. He tucked his shirt into his trousers, and was fighting in the ranks again before I had capped my rifle. The ball had cut a groove in his skin only. The play of this Irishman's face was so expressive, his emotions changed so quickly, that I could not keep from laughing.

Near Spottsylvania I saw, as my battery was moving into action, a group of wounded men lying in the shade cast by some large oak trees. All of these men's faces were gray. They silently looked at us as we marched past them. One wounded man, a blond giant of about forty years, was smoking a short briar-wood pipe. He had a firm grip on the pipe-stem. I asked him what he was doing. " Having my last smoke, young fellow," he replied. His dauntless blue eyes met mine, and he bravely tried to smile. I saw that he was dying fast. Another of these wounded men was trying to read a letter. He was too weak to hold it, or maybe his sight was clouded. He thrust it unread into the breast pocket of his blouse, and lay back with a moan. This group of wounded men numbered fifteen or twenty. At the time, I thought that all of them were fatally wounded, and that there was no use in the surgeons wasting time on them, when men who could be saved were clamoring for their skilful attention. None of these soldiers cried aloud, none called on wife, or mother, or father. They lay on the ground, pale-faced, and with set jaws, waiting for their end. They moaned and groaned as they suffered, but none of them flunked. When my battery returned from the front, five or six hours afterward, almost all of these men were dead. Long before the campaign was over I concluded that dying soldiers seldom called on those who were dearest to them, seldom conjured their Northern on Southern homes, until they became delirious. Then, when their minds wandered, and fluttered at the approach of freedom, they babbled of their homes. Some were boys again, and were fishing in Northern trout streams. Some were generals leading their men to victory. Some were with their wives and children. Some wandered over their family's homestead ; but all, with rare exceptions, were delirious.

At the North Anna River, my battery being in action, an infantry soldier, one of our supports, who was lying face downward close behind the gun I served on, and in a place where he thought he was safe, was struck on the thighs by a large jagged piece of a shell. The wound made by this fragment of iron was as horrible as any I saw in the army. The flesh of both thighs was torn off, exposing the bones. The soldier bled to death in a few minutes, and before he died he conjured his Northern home, and murmured of his wife and children.

In the same battle, but on the south side of the river, a man who carried a rifle was passing between the guns and caissons of the battery. A solid shot, intended for us, struck him on the side. His entire bowels were torn out and slung in ribbons and shreds on the ground. He fell dead, but his arms and legs jerked convulsively a few times. It was a sickening spectacle. During this battle I saw a Union picket knocked down, probably by a rifle-ball striking his head and glancing from it. He lay as though dead. Presently he struggled to his feet, and with blood streaming from his head, he staggered aimlessly round and round in a circle, as sheep afflicted with grubs in the brain do. Instantly the Confederate sharp-shooters opened fire on him and speedily killed him as he circled.

Wounded soldiers almost always tore their clothing away from their wounds, so as to see them and to judge of their character. Many of them would smile and their faces would brighten as they realized that they were not hard hit, and that they could go home for a few months. Others would give a quick glance at their wounds and then shrink back as from a blow, and turn pale, as they realized the truth that they were mortally wounded. The enlisted men were exceedingly accurate judges of the probable result which would ensue from any wound they saw. They had seen hundreds of soldiers wounded, and they had noticed that certain wounds always resulted fatally. They knew when they were fatally wounded, and after the shock of discovery had passed, they generally braced themselves and died in a manly manner. It was seldom that an American or Irish volunteer flunked in the presence of death.

XII.

EARLY IN FRONT OF WASHINGTON.

MY experience as an enlisted man during Grant's last campaign ended when I left City Point, Virginia. I write this and the succeeding chapters to present certain conditions and facts in the war, which fell within my personal experience, and which, I think, merit permanent record.

I arrived in Washington June 25, 1864, and re-enlisted in the United States Army the same day. I spent six days in my father's house, sleeping and fighting off fever. On June 30th, I was appointed Second Lieutenant in the Fourth United States Artillery, and a verbal leave of absence was granted to me by Secretary of War Stanton, whom I found, contrary to my expectation, to be a very kind and pleasant-spoken gentleman.

About July 1st, a rumor circulated through Washington that our troops had met with a

serious disaster in the neighborhood of Mar-
tinsburg. Then men whispered one to the
other that a large Confederate army was rava-
ging the southern border of Pennsylvania, and
that Washington was threatened. There was
great uneasiness in the capitol. President Lincoln called on the States of New York, Pennsylvania, and Massachusetts for troops to aid in
repelling the invasion. The rumors grew
thicker and thicker, and all of them were un-
favorable to the Union cause. The only report
we could rely on was that Early's corps, of the
Army of Northern Virginia, had been detached
by Lee to drive the Union forces out of Shenandoah Valley, to ravage Southern Pennsylvania, and to capture the national capitol, if
possible. Washington was in an uproar. In
the morning we heard that Early was at a certain point. At night he was reported as being
fifty miles from there. To-day his army was
alleged to number 30,000 men. On the morrow,
pale-faced, anxious men solemnly asserted that
certain information had been received at the
War Department that at least 50,000 veteran
soldiers were marching with Early. Late at
night on July 9th, I was sitting in Willard's
Hotel. An excited man walked rapidly in and

told the group in which I was talking, that our army, under General Lew Wallace, had been disastrously defeated on the Monocacy by Early, and that our disordered troops were in full retreat on Baltimore. Later we heard that Wallace's army had been annihilated. Still later that the government's books, records, and money were being packed in boxes preparatory to its flight to New York. Almost every man I met that night believed that the Confederate guns would be thundering at the capital in less than twenty-four hours.

The next morning the report of our defeat on the Monocacy was confirmed, and the excitement in the city grew more and more intense. Men stood in groups on street corners, in hotel lobbies, in newspaper offices, and in drinking saloons, and discussed the military situation. Officers rode furiously up and down the streets, and swarmed around the War Department. I began to think that maybe Early would make a dash at Washington. So I walked to the War Department and reported for duty. I was greatly astonished at the authentic news I heard. War Department officials told me that General Auger, who had command of the troops at Washington, did not have 5,000 stanch, veteran soldiers with which to defend the entire line, which was about thirty miles long. He had a few 100-day men, a few quartermaster employés, and some disabled soldiers, called veteran reserves. I was assured that a successful defence of the city could not be made, unless reinforcements speedily arrived. Finally I was ordered to report for duty to the commanding officer of Battery A Fourth United States Artillery, then in garrison at Fort Totten, near Bladensburg.

Arrived at the fort, I found it was commanded by a captain of a 100-day regiment from Ohio, and that the regular army artillerists were under his orders. This Ohio captain carried matters with a light hand. He was anxious to be advised, and cheerfully allowed the artillery officers to do as they thought best in all matters relative to the defence of the fort. Battery A was commanded by handsome, songful Rufus King. Howard B. Cushing, a brother of the "Gettysburg" and the "Albemarle" Cushings, was a second lieutenant in this battery. It had been serving with Custer as horse artillery, and had been badly cut up in front of Richmond, and had been sent to Washington for rest. Neither the officers nor the men understood handling the large guns with which the fort was armed.   On the parade ground within the fort were six brass James guns.   We quickly decided to use these in the threatened battle. The magazine was opened.   Barrels of powder were brought out and rolled up and down, and placed in the sunshine to thoroughly dry. Shot and shell and stands of grape were brought out, and all hands made cartridges for the 100-pound Parrotts, and assorted the ammunition for the James guns, which were placed in position on the side of the fort which we expected to be attacked.

Late in the afternoon, July 10th, word was sent to us from Washington that Early was marching with his entire army on the capital, and that he was then near Rockville.   That evening the motliest crowd of soldiers I ever saw came straggling out from Washington to man the rifle-pits which connected the forts.   This force was composed of quartermaster's employés, clerks from the War, Navy, and State departments, convalescents from the military hospitals, and veteran reserves, the latter clad in the disheartening, sickly uniform of pale blue, which was the distinctive dress of that corps. (The Confederates aptly characterized these

disabled soldiers as "Condemned Yankees.")
There was little order or discipline among these
pretended soldiers. The sturdy Irishmen who
manned our guns and who had been forged into
perfect soldiers by "Gettysburg" Cushing,
gazed at them with open-eyed astonishment.
They gabbled, and were evidently trying to
keep up their courage by talking loudly and
boastfully of their determination to hold the
rifle-pits at all hazards. I smiled sorrowfully
as I thought of the ease with which the Confederates, veterans of twenty pitched-battles,
would drive them out of their earthworks.
The 100-day men who were in the fort were
somewhat nervous; but they meant to fight,
and when they had been warmed in battle fire,
and men had begun to fall, they undoubtedly
would have fought stanchly.

That night, King, Cushing, and I slept on
the top of the magazine, and the cannoneers
slept on the ground by their guns. Early the
next morning we saw that a signal-station had
been established on the top of the Soldiers'
Home, and that officers of the signal corps
were furiously waving flags to communicate information to head-quarters. We knew that
important news was being waved through the

air, but we could not read the signals. So we began to search through our field-glasses for the Confederate soldiers. We found them soon. A body of Confederate cavalry rode aimlessly to and fro along the edge of a wood, about five miles from our fort. We saw their artillery glisten in the sun. Soon smoke began to rise in heavy columns behind them, and I knew that they were burning houses. That afternoon the Confederate infantry came in sight, and formed a battle line. Portions of this line were within range of some of the forts, and heavy guns opened on it away off to our left. This artillery practice, marked by the bursting shells, was the poorest I ever saw. It was evident that the department clerks or the 100-day men were serving the guns. The Confederates did not pay the slightest attention to this fire. Their skirmishers, a cloud of them, advanced a short distance from their main line, and then sank out of sight.

We grew anxious. I knew that Early, who had about eighteen thousand veteran soldiers with him, could break our line whenever he saw fit to strike it. I knew that he could capture Washington in two hours, if he determined to take the national capital. How

we fumed and fretted ! Before sunrise on July
12th we saw that Early's men were in motion.
They moved slowly toward our intrenchments,
with a heavy line of skirmishers preceding their
battle line. These skirmishers drove our pickets before them with great ease. The Confederate battle line advanced until they were
within long-cannon range of the forts. Their
skirmishers were within rifle range, and Confederate bullets occasionally sang above us.
Many heavy guns opened on the battle line.
It halted, and the men lay down in the grass,
among bushes, and behind buildings. Ammunition was in plentiful supply in Fort Totten,
and we manned three one-hundred-pound Par-
rott guns, and wasted a ton of shells to get the
range and to burn a few vision-obscuring houses
which stood on the ground over which we expected the charge to be made. Through our
glasses we could see the disposition of Early's
troops. We three young artillery officers sat
on the magazine and studied his line. We
speedily saw that his troops were not formed
in charging column ; saw that there was no reserve ; saw that there was no eager hurrying to
and fro of soldiers ; saw that there was no preparatory bustle ; saw, that though the Confed-

erate skirmishers were far in advance of the main line, they were not pushing our pickets, and were not firing with earnestness. Evidently there was to be no serious fighting that morning. We continued to shell the Confederate line without a particle of effect, unless to excite the contempt of veteran soldiers.

Toward evening General Auger drew a heavy body of troops from our thin defensive line, and sent them out to feel of Early's men. Naturally the latter objected to being felt of. So they promptly killed and wounded three hundred of Auger's men. These having had enough of dallying with savage-tempered and veteran Confederate infantry, skurried back to our intrenchments.

Next morning opened with a heavy fire from the forts to our left, and more houses were burned. The position of the Confederate pickets, marked by rifle flashes and tiny puffs of powder-smoke, was apparently unchanged ; but their main line had been drawn back to the shelter of the woods. We were anxiously debating the question : " Is Early forming his soldiers into a charging column ? " when we heard a clatter of galloping horses, and a signal corps officer and two enlisted men rode up to the gate of the fort and demanded admittance. Admitted, they clambered on to the magazine. Eager for news, we assailed the officer with questions. He told us that the Union people in Washington had been panic-stricken; that the government had been ready to leave the city; that the money and books had been packed preparatory to shipment north; that the majority of the masculine portion of the entire city had got wildly drunk and kept so; and that the Sixth Corps was coming up the Potomac River to the defence of Washington. He began to wave his flags. The signal flags on top of the Soldiers' Home waved back in answer, and as they waved the signal officer slowly read out the message, word by word: "Transports loaded with troops in sight." About seven o'clock the flags which were on top of the Soldiers' Home waved briskly. The signal corps officer answered an inquiring look by reading aloud: "Sixth Corps disembarking. Troops marching for the front." Now we were as anxious for Early to assault our works, as we had been fearful of his doing so the previous day. We had the Sixth Corps, stanch, determined fighters, at our backs. We were no longer fearful of our supports running away in panic. Again the flags waved. Again the signal officer read to us: "Infantry turned into Seventh Street. All troops marching to the front." I could have hugged that signal corps officer. He rolled up his flags, bade us good day, and smilingly said: "Gentlemen, you are saved from the mortification of losing your fort. And, thank God! Washington is saved from capture." He turned, mounted his horse, and rode out of the fort.

Down the road, away past the Soldiers' Home, we heard faint strains of martial music. Then we saw a column of dust rising. It rose high above the trees, high above the houses. Then its head was thrust into sight, a few dust-obscured officers riding in advance, the dust sloping upward and backward from them. Close behind them came a large banner, blazoned with a great crimson cross. It was the flag of the First Division of the Sixth Corps. Clouds of dust rolled heavily upward, almost obscuring it at times, but I watched it intently, and my throat filled, and my heart thumped. The Confederate skirmishers disappeared. The Sixth Corps marched on to the battle-ground, formed line, and, preceded by hundreds of skirmishers, advanced. Alas, too late! The last Confederates had hastened after their leader, and were well on their way to the Shenandoah Valley.

Could Early have captured Washington on June 11–12, 1864? I unhesitatingly answer, yes. I supplement this by saying that he could have taken the city without losing more than one thousand men. But if he had taken it, his poorly clad, poorly fed, impoverished men would inevitably have gone to plundering, would inevitably have gotten drunk and stayed drunk, and he would have lost his entire army.

XIII.

THE MILITARY PRISON AT ELMIRA.

AFTER General Early had withdrawn his soldiers from the front of Washington, Battery A Fourth United States Artillery joined the artillery reserve then lying in Camp Barry, near Washington. Life in Camp Barry was exceedingly monotonous, and enlisted men and officers alike were impatient to be ordered to active service. There was joy in the camp, one afternoon in late fall, when an order came, directing the commanding officer of Battery A to go at once to Elmira, New York, with a section of artillery, and to report for duty to the commanding officer of that post. The senior lieutenant, Rufus King, was absent on leave. Lieutenant Cushing, eager to get out of Washington, ordered me to get a section in marching order. I did so, and we marched to the railroad station, and loaded the guns, caissons, and horses on the cars, and left Washington in less than two hours after receiving the order.

We had heard that the Confederate soldiers who were confined in the military prison at Elmira were somewhat unruly, and next day, when we reported for duty to a 100-day colonel, we were not surprised to hear that the prisoners were insubordinate, and that an outbreak was imminent. We marched the battery to the military prison. There we found about twelve thousand Confederate prisoners, who were confined in a large stockade, inside of which were many barracks, and through which the Chemung River flowed. The stockade, made of logs set deeply in the ground on end and standing side by side, was about twelve feet high. About four feet below the top of the stockade, on the outside, was a platform, guarded by a handrail, which extended around the prison. This platform was studded by sentry-boxes at short intervals. On it sentinels walked to and fro, day and night, and watched the prisoners. During the night they, at half hour intervals, loudly called the number to their post, and announced that all was well. It was almost dark when we arrived at the prison, and we parked the guns in an open space near the stockade. Around us were many camps, which were occupied by disorderly, undrilled 100-day men. We speedily discovered that there was a lack of discipline in the prison. The Confederates were ugly-tempered and rebellious. That night they gathered in mobs, and the Confederate charging-yell rang out clearly. They threw stones at the sentinels. They refused to go into their barracks. Evidently they knew that the men who guarded them were not soldiers. The uproar increased in volume. I was confident that the prisoners intended to break out that night. Our guns were placed in battery, and the ammunition chests opened. We waited, and waited, and waited, and finally I rode over to an infantry camp in search of information, and there found a 100-day colonel, who was playing cribbage with a sergeant. I asked the meaning of the uproar in the prison, and the colonel said, indifferently: "Oh, that is nothing! They generally make twice as much noise," and he continued to move his pegs up and down the cribbage-board. I returned to camp greatly disgusted.

The next day Cushing and I went into the prison, and after carefully examining it, concluded that if an attempt to break guard was

made it would be directed against the point
where the river left the stockade. As we
walked slowly around the prison, groups of
Confederates looked curiously at us and talked
insultingly about us. One crowd of men followed us to the river bank and jeered us as we inspected the stockade there. Cushing lost his
temper and turned savagely to face them, and
said in a low, clear voice : " See here, — — —!
I am just up from the front, where I have been
killing such infernal wretches as you are. I have
met you in twenty battles. I never lost a gun
to you. You never drove a battery I served
with from its position. You are a crowd of insolent, cowardly scoundrels, and if I had command of this prison I would discipline you,
or kill you, and I should much prefer to kill
you. I have brought a battery of United
States artillery to this pen, and if you will
give me occasion I will be glad to dam that
river," pointing to the Chemung, "with your
worthless carcasses, and silence your insolent
tongues forever. I fully understand that you
are presuming on your position as prisoners of
war when you talk to me as you have ; but,"
and here his hand shook warningly in the faces
of the group, "you have reached the end of

your rope with me. I will kill the first man of you who again speaks insultingly to me while I am in this pen, and I shall be here daily. Now, go to your quarters." And they went. We returned to our camp, moved the guns to a position which commanded the river, and then rearranged the ammunition, putting all the canister in the chests of the gun limbers. And then we waited for the expected outbreak.

A military prison, it matters not what people keep it, is not a place where life is enjoyed. The prisoners are enemies, and their keepers care but little for their lives or comfort. It is probable that we fed the Confederate prisoners better than they fed Union prisoners. Personally I know nothing of life in Confederate military prisons, as I was not captured. I saw many thousands of our soldiers shortly after they were exchanged. By far the larger portion of these men were in good condition and fit for service. It is true that many of them were diseased and almost dead when they were delivered to us, and these soldiers were grouped and photographed, very unfairly I think, and the illustrated papers which reproduced these photographs were widely circulated throughout the Northern States. I met no Union soldier who had been confined in a Confederate military prison, who thought it to be a pleasant retreat; and I know that the military prison at Elmira was a place to be avoided by men of good taste. The prisoners, it was alleged, were allowed the same rations, excepting coffee and sugar, that their guards received. They did not get it. I repeatedly saw the Confederate prisoners draw their provisions, and they never got more than two thirds rations. Many of them were diseased, many were slightly wounded, many were feeble and worn out with campaigning in Virginia, and many more were home-sick; and these men died as sheep with the rot. Almost daily a wagon piled high with pine coffins entered the stockade, and these coffins were filled with dead Confederates. The sound men, the men of vigorous constitution, and those possessing aggressive minds, endured prison life without suffering greatly; and this I suspect was true of Union soldiers confined in Confederate prisons. The winter of 1864–65 was exceedingly cold. The Confederate prisoners, thinly clad, enfeebled by campaigning, and further weakened by insufficient supplies of food, were unable to endure the cold of a Northern winter. They died by the hundred. They were mentally depressed, and the inevitable result followed. Their wounds became gangrenous and they died; they were home-sick and they died; they contracted pneumonia and died. Fever stalked among them and struck hundreds of them down. Bowel disorders carried off other hundreds. I have seen groups of battle-worn, home-sick Confederates, their thin blankets drawn tightly around their shoulders, stand in the lee of a barrack for an hour without speaking to one another. They stood motionless and gazed into one another's haggard faces with despairing eyes. There was no need to talk, as all topics of conversation had long since been exhausted.

The majority of the prisoners were exceedingly ignorant. Many of them could not read or write. I often admired the military skill displayed by the Confederate officers in forging these ignorant men into the almost perfect soldiers they were. The discipline in the Confederate armies must have been exceedingly severe to have enabled their officers to control these reckless, savage-tempered men. The prisoners at Elmira were exclusively Americans. I did not see a foreign-born citizen in that prison. These soldiers were penniless.

They could not buy clothing or articles of prime necessity. They were eager to work, to earn money to buy tobacco. On pleasant days a few hundred of them were employed outside the stockade in digging ditches and trenches which were never used. For this work they were paid about twenty-five cents per day, which sum they promptly invested in tobacco. I have seen the prisoners display as much eagerness to secure this employment, as free men would to secure remunerative positions of trust. And they worked faithfully and honestly, and earned their scanty pay. Thinly clad, with their blankets wound around them instead of overcoats, poorly fed, hopeless, these unfortunate soldiers swung heavy picks, and bent low over their shovels, as the cold wind swept through their emaciated frames as through a sieve. It was pitiful to see the poverty-stricken Confederates breaking the hard, frost-bound earth, while armed sentinels passed to and fro about them, and a battery of artillery moved swiftly over the frozen plain in menacing drill.

Outside of the stockade, and on the other side of the road, two tall wooden towers had been built by some enterprising Yankees. The owners of these buildings made a profitable show of the Confederate prisoners. Daily their tops were thronged with curious spectators, who paid ten cents each to look into the prison pen. A few weeks after these towers were built, I noticed that a young and handsome woman visited one of them daily, and waved her handkerchief frequently. It was evident to me that she was communicating with the prisoners, probably to her friends or relatives who were confined in the stockade. One night seven or eight Confederates escaped from the prison by crawling through a tunnel that they had dug, and were seen no more. I was exceedingly glad that these men had escaped. The young woman disappeared also. Then I reported what I had seen, and the towers were closed by military orders.

One night the uproar in the stockade was terrific. A rifle shot rang out clearly. I heard a sentinel on post call for the officer of the guard. The long roll sounded in the infantry camps. The noise of infantry falling into line hummed in the air. The night was intensely dark. I stood in the door of my tent listening to the uproar in the Confederate pen. I judged that the prisoners were divided into two groups; one standing by the river bank, the other near the gate. Both groups were yelling at the top of their voices. Some of the soldiers of the regular brigade, which had been sent from the Army of the Potomac to assist in guarding the prisoners, were on duty that night. And I heard these cool veterans caution the Confederates not to cross the dead-line, and to repeatedly tell them to stand back or they would fire on them. Another shot rang out clearly. My battery bugler, a Jew, named Samuels, came to me, bugle in hand. " Blow Boots and Saddles," I said. Instantly the artillery camp was alive. Half-dressed men sprang to the guns, horses were harnessed and saddled. I called an old sergeant to me and said : " Trail No. 2 gun on the stockade near the river, and if the prisoners break out, dose the head of the column with double canister until they run over your gun. Fire a blank cartridge to summon Lieutenant Cushing and the enlisted men, who are in town, to the battery. I will take No. 1 gun close to the stockade and smash the flank of the column to flinders if it comes out. I will burn a lantern by the gun so as to mark my position." The sergeant moved off in the darkness. I saw the flash of his gun, heard a shot scream close above my head, and then heard the crash of timber as the shot tore through a barrack, and this was followed by cries of alarm. I heard the Confederates cry: " Look out, the artillery has opened!" Instantly the uproar ceased. The great prison was as silent as death, and instantly I knew I was in a scrape, and would probably be court-martialed for firing on the prisoners. Out of town came Cushing, his horse in a lather. I explained to him what had happened. He looked soberly at me for an instant, and then said : "You will be court-martialed, sure. You must get to your own battery at once (I belonged to Battery H), and get off before the 100-day officers prefer charges against you. Then we can talk them out of it." An officer from head-quarters rode up and complained bitterly of the outrage of firing on the prisoners. From him we learned that it was a stone instead of a shot that had been fired into the prison. Early the next morning I left Elmira, having been ordered by a speedily procured telegram to join Battery H, Fourth United States Artillery, in the department of the Cumberland. I afterwards learned that a few Confederates were wounded by splinters when the stone struck the barrack, and that they never again made night hideous by their yells and howls.

XIV.

IN THE SOUTHWEST.

WHEN I arrived at Nashville, Tennessee, I was told that my battery was at the front, probably near Stevenson, Alabama. I went to that town, and there met Lieutenant John Stevenson, Fourth United States Artillery, whose temper was as sunny as his hair, and he told me that my battery was with the Fourth Corps, then marching on Huntsville, Alabama, but that the corps could not possibly arrive there for two or three days. Stevenson invited me to stay with him for a day, and I accepted his invitation.

At Stevenson there was a large refugee camp, where many women and children and a few crippled or age-enfeebled men had sought refuge from attacks by murderous bands of guerrillas. The camp had probably been abandoned when Hood swept north with his army, and the refugees had sought shelter and food as best they could.   Hood's army went to pieces after being defeated at Nashville, and the refugees again gathered at Stevenson. Guerrillas infested the southern highlands. These pretended soldiers, it mattered not which uniform they disgraced by wearing, were, almost without exception, robbers and murderers, who sought to enrich themselves by plundering their defenceless neighbors.   They rode through the southern highlands, killing men, burning houses, stealing cattle and horses. To-day a band of guerrillas, alleged Unionists, ravaged a mountain district.   They killed their personal enemies, whom they said were Confederate sympathizers, and destroyed their property.   To-morrow other guerrillas burned Union men's houses, and shot so-called Union men to death.   This relentless, mountain warfare was exceedingly hard on women and children.   Agriculture was suspended in the highlands.   No man dared to till his lean fields for fear that some hidden enemy might kill him. No stack of unthrashed grain or garner of corn was safe from the torch.   The defenceless women and children were starved out of their homes, and they sought safety and food within the Union lines.   Our government established

extensive camps for these war-stricken Southerners.

Curious to see these people I spent a day in
camp at Stevenson. I saw hundreds of tall,
gaunt, frouzy-headed, snuff-dipping, pipe-smok-
ing, unclean women. Some were clad in homespun stuffs, others in calico, others in bagging.
Many of them were unshod. There were hundreds and hundreds of vermin-infested and supremely dirty children in the camp. Some
families lived in tents, some in flimsy barracks.
All lived in discomfort. All drew rations from
the government. All were utterly poor. It
seemed that they were too poor to ever again
get a start in life. Haggard, wind- and sun-
and storm-burnt women, their gaunt forms
showing plainly through their rags, sat, or
lolled, or stood in groups, talking drawlingly.
Their features were as expressionless as wood,
their eyes lustreless. I talked to many of
these women. All told stories of murder, of
arson, of blood-curdling scenes. One, gray-
eyed, bony, square-jawed, barefooted, forty
years old, clad in a dirty, ragged, homespun
dress, sat on a log outside of a tent sucking a
corn-cob pipe. Her tow-headed children played
around her. She told me that before the war

she and her husband owned a mountain farm, where they lived in comfort ; that they owned horses, cattle, and pigs, and raised plenty of corn and tobacco. One day her husband, who was a Union man, was shot dead as he stood by her side in the door of their house. She buried him in a grave she dug herself. She and her children tended the crops. These were burned shortly after they gathered them. Then her swine were stolen, and her cows and horse driven off. Finally her oldest son, a boy of fourteen, was shot dead at the spring, and her house and barn were burned in broad daylight, and she and her children were left homeless and without food on a desolate mountain side. Many of her neighbors had been burned out the same day. They joined forces and wandered down the mountain, hungry, cold, with little children tugging at women's dresses, to a Union camp. From there they had been sent to Stevenson. Long before this woman had finished her story she rose to her feet, her face was white with intense passion, her eyes blazed with fire, and her gaunt form quivered with excitement as she gesticulated savagely. She said that if she lived, and her boys lived, that she would have vengeance on the men who had murdered her husband and son, and destroyed her home. As she talked so talked all. These women were saturating their children's minds with the stories of the wrongs they had endured. I heard them repeat over and over to their children the names of men which they were never to forget, and whom they were to kill when they had sufficient strength to hold a rifle. The stolid manners, the wooden faces, the lustreless eyes, the drawling speech of these people, concealed the volcanoes of fire and wrath which burned within their breasts. One woman dramatically described the death of her husband. The puff of powder smoke curling above the clump of laurel, the reeling man with blood gushing from his mouth, the digging of his grave, the midnight burial,—all were pictured. These women, who had been driven from their homes by the most savage warfare our country has been cursed with, knew what war was, and they impressed me as living wholly to revenge their wrongs. It was easy to foresee the years of bloodshed, of assassination, of family feuds, that would spring from the recollections of the war, handed from widowed mothers to savage-tempered sons, in the mountain recesses of Georgia, Tennessee, Alabama, and Kentucky.

And long after the war closed rifles continued to crack in remote mountain glens, as the open accounts between families were settled.

I started for Huntsville the next morning. The railroad was dilapidated. Tiny columns of mud spouted in the air as the wheels rolled over the splintered rails. The train consisted of open and box cars, which were loaded with veteran soldiers returning to their commands. These soldiers were almost without exception Americans, and were reckless and apparently indifferent to danger. Two or three piles of clay were thrown on each car, and the men tramped it into rough hearths, about a foot thick and four feet square, and built fires on them. Around these fires the soldiers crowded to cook their rations. At every station the supply of firewood we carried was added to. The bottom of the cars charred and holes were formed. I expected the train to catch fire and burn. The soldiers sang wild and profane songs, and kept time by sounding their ramrods in their musket barrels, or by softly tapping them with steel bayonets. It began to rain and the wind blew strongly. These soldiers, exposed to the storm on open cars, built their fires higher and sang tunefully through it. They were courageous, imaginative, reckless Western American volunteers, an entirely different race of men from their Eastern brothers.

About midnight the train halted at Paint Rock River (the railroad bridge which spanned that stream had been burned by guerrillas the previous night, and some scores of army bridge-builders were at work to replace it) and the soldiers clambered off of the cars. They built fires on the bank of the rapid, swollen stream, and then, without an instant's hesitation, began to build a raft, on which to cross the river. I was greatly impressed by the self-reliant manhood of these enlisted men. When the raft was finished a number of men crowded on it and poled it across the river. Fires by which to see were built on the other side. The raft was poled to and fro and the troops were slowly ferried across. Eager to cross, to get near to their regiments, they frequently overloaded the raft and it sank deeply in the water. Then the soldiers would spring ashore or fall into the river, out of which they swam, or were pulled by their comrades. The result was inevitable. On the sixth trip the raft was loaded so heavily that the water was over the shoes of the soldiers. It was safely poled to the middle of the stream. There it tilted, and with a howl the soldiers slid into the water. Most of them swam ashore, rifle in hand, or clambered back on the raft. But I saw five men, who were heavily laden with cartridges or could not swim, sink into the cold water to be seen no more. The men who had clambered on the raft poled it back to shore and called for another cargo, and other men swarmed on to the perilous craft. No one paid the slightest attention to the drowned men. I saw that I could not get across the river for hours, so I hung my rubber blanket over a bush and sat under it to watch the scene. The wind had ceased to blow, and the rain fell gently. Great fires of logs and railroad ties burned brightly. Scores of bridge-builders worked in torch-relieved darkness. Another train loaded with troops came up, and these men rushed to the river's bank. A thousand soldiers were grouped at the river, and as they stood in the rain they sang " John Brown " and kept time with sounding rifles. The two empty trains backed off. Presently another train thundered down the railroad track, and stopped on a high, rocky embankment directly in front of me. It was loaded with escaped negro slaves, who had fled from many cotton plantations, and who had burdened themselves with plunder stolen from their masters' houses. The train hands, who were soldiers, roughly hustled the negroes from the train and carelessly threw their baggage after them. Trunks, boxes, costly articles of furniture, and rolls of blankets and clothing were thrown down the embankment, rolling, slowly at first, then faster and faster, to the bottom. Many trunks and boxes leaped high in the air and struck heavily on rocks when they descended. These burst open and their contents were scattered. Excited negroes chased their boxes down the embankment, to be frightened and confused by other boxes bounding past them. Black men howled ; black women screamed ; black babies cried. After the destruction of personal property had ceased, these wretched, rain-soaked people gathered their effects as best they could and straggled off into the forest. There presently fires glowed.

Next day I arrived at Huntsville. At headquarters I was told that my battery was probably serving with General Wilson's cavalry, and that he and General Thomas were supposed to be somewhere in Northern Mississippi. I se-

cured orders and transportation, and promptly
started back to Nashville on an open box car.
The train stopped in a forest to take on wood,
which was piled at a side track. The conduc-
tor told me that the train would stay on the
side track for three or four hours. I picked up
my blankets, jumped off the car, and walked into the sunny forest. The locomotive's whistle
sounded. The train rolled off. The enlisted
men jeered me. I was in no hurry, and rather
enjoyed the situation. The Alabama woods
were pleasant. I would wait for the next train.
Noon came. Late in the afternoon I resolved
to walk to the next station, where I knew
Union soldiers were on guard. While I was
at Huntsville I had learned that the region I
was in was infested with guerillas, at the head
of whom was a murderous ruffian, named Dick
Cotton. This man was described to be wholly
devilish. It was alleged that he murdered every
Union soldier that fell into his hands, and
that he invariably acted on the maxim that
dead men tell no tales. As I walked with
uneven steps on the ties, the stories I had
heard of Dick Cotton and his band of murderers filled my brain. To my right was a high,
precipitous mountain range. The whole region

seemed to be deserted. Darkness, gray and gloomy, began to gather in the forest. I heard a flock of wild turkeys calling one another. Then I saw them walk briskly among the trees. Seeing me they ran swiftly out of sight. The sun sank behind the mountains. To my right I saw a column of smoke rising out of a ravine. I left the railroad track and walked through the forest to the ravine. While walking, I crossed a heavy bridle path which led up the gulch, and presumably across the mountain. A small, dilapidated log-house and a few out-buildings stood in a cleared field in the ravine. There were neither dogs nor chickens around this place. I walked slowly to the door of the house and knocked. A surly, gray-haired, savage-faced white man opened it. Under his left armpit was a rude crutch. He looked at me with fiery eyes as I stated my case, and then gruffly bade me enter. A yellow negro man, whom I saw was the son of the white man, sat on the stool before the fire cooking supper. The manner of my host changed. He smiled and talked and endeavored to simulate good comradeship. I instantly realized that I was in danger. The yellow man could not conceal his hostility. After supper I heard a horse stamp

in one of the out-buildings. My host continued
to smile and talk of the times before the war,
and of his plantation in the valley below, where
he had worked twenty slaves in productive
cotton fields. He told how they had all run
away, excepting the boy (a broad-shouldered
man of thirty years) who still served him ; and
he prated about the wickedness of war, and of
his gladness that it was almost over, and the
useless shedding of fraternal blood near its end.
As he talked, his cruel black eyes gleamed with
hostility and belied his words. I turned to
speak to the slave, who sat smoking and blow-
ing his tobacco-smoke up the chimney, and saw
that he was furtively watching his master, and
out of the tail of my eye I saw the white man
jerk his left thumb toward the door, motioning
to the slave to go outside. Soon the negro
arose and went out, after firewood he said.
Presently my host arose, excused himself,
placed his crutch under his arm, and said : " I
must go see what keeps that lazy nigger." He
stumped across the floor, opened the door, and
went out, leaving the door slightly ajar behind
him. I walked softly across the floor and
listened with keen ear at the crack. I heard
him whisper to the slave: "Charles, saddle

the mare, ride across the mountain and tell Mr. Cotton that there is a — — — Yankee artillery officer here, and tell him to come get him." That was precisely what I had been expecting. I drew my heavy revolver, silently cocked it, then threw the door wide open and instantly covered the typical Southern planter and his yellow son, and said : "Come in here, you damned villains, or I will kill both of you." They sullenly re-entered the house, and sat on two chairs in a corner for the remainder of the night, while I sat by the fire. The night was long. Conversation lagged. I thought morning would never come. When it did come my host and his yellow son and I took a walk before breakfast. They preceded me down the railroad track for two miles. There I bade them farewell and walked briskly to the next station, where I found a detachment of an Illinois regiment, which was commanded by a young sergeant, who gave me a welcome and a breakfast. I have told this incident simply to illustrate the feeling of the small and ignorant Southern planters,—men who owned a few slaves, and who knew that they would be ruined by the suppression of the slaveholders' rebellion.

Arrived at Nashville I was ordered to report to the chief of artillery of the Army of the Cumberland, at Eastport, Mississippi. I went to Paduka, Kentucky, and took steamer up the Tennessee River. This boat was loaded with provisions and soldiers returning from furlough. Going up the Tennessee River in a steamboat was not as monotonous then as it is now. Guerrillas and bushwhackers lurked in the forests which bordered the river. The pilot-houses of all boats which plied the river were protected with heavy boiler-plate iron to keep out Confederate rifle-balls. Southern sympathizers amused themselves, and served their cause, by endeavoring to kill the pilots of the steamboats, so as to wreck them. Daily we saw many men, clad in homespun, skulking in the forest. They dodged from tree to tree. They lay behind stumps and logs. They knew the forest trails. They could not be captured. Puffs of powder smoke would shoot forth from behind trees or out of dense thickets, and frequently the balls would enter the pilot-house through unprotected windows in front. The pilots did not wince. They said that they received large pay, and that part of their duty was to serve as targets for skulking sharp-

shooters. When unwary soldiers exposed themselves, they were promptly fired at, and occasionally shot. Then their comrades would rush
on deck and fire scores of shots at the place
where the bushwhacker was last seen. Presently there would be a puff of smoke from another
point. Then all the soldiers would shoot at
that point. Daily soldiers were killed and
wounded on the steamer. I do not believe
that a single bushwhacker was shot, and thousands of balls were shot at them. The farther
south we went, the more numerous were the
lurking sharp-shooters.

I found the Army of the Cumberland at
Eastport, and reported for duty. I was amazed
to learn that my battery, H of the Fourth
Artillery, had been sent East, to Camp Barry,
at Washington, a month before I left Elmira!
While I was talking to the chief of artillery,
General Thomas entered the tent, and smiled
kindly at my rage. He ordered transportation
to be furnished to me from Eastport to Washington, and that I be ordered there at once.

I had travelled on an order from Elmira,
New York, by car, by steamer, on horseback,
and on foot, for thousands of miles, through
many States, searching for a battery of artillery

which was all the while at Washington, and whose commander daily expected me to appear. I never heard of the War Department officials being mistaken as to the location of any other command during the entire war.

I returned to Washington, and there saw the great army of volunteers melt away. The men with whom I had served had gone to work in the fields, in the shops, in mills, and in factories. I had no interest in the regular army, no desire to continue to loaf around barracks, and to drill foreign-born soldiers. So I resigned my commission and went home.

END